THE HEART IS THE CENTER OF THE UNIVERSE

LAURA LIVIA GRIGORE

Thought Catalog Books
Brooklyn, NY

THOUGHT CATALOG BOOKS

Copyright © 2015 by Laura Livia Grigore. All rights reserved. Published by Thought Catalog Books, a division of The Thought & Expression Co., Williamsburg, Brooklyn. For general information and submissions: manuscripts@thoughtcatalog.com.

    First edition, 2015.
    ISBN 978-0692601594
    10 9 8 7 6 5 4 3 2 1

Founded in 2010, Thought Catalog is a website and imprint dedicated to your ideas and stories. We publish fiction and non-fiction from emerging and established writers across all genres.

Cover image by © iStock.com/Bashutskyy
Cover design and layout by KJ Parish

To I

THE LOVE STORIES

THE DIFFERENCE BETWEEN TRUE LOVE AND OBSESSION IS REALITY

Love, if not shared, one cannot call love. Call it the memory of love or the longing for love. Or even better, obsession. It happened to all of us, no matter how cool, intelligent and loveable we think we are.

Is unrequited love, the dramatic, intense and eventually painful type of love, just an obsession? I kept thinking about this lately.

I remember a talk I had many years ago with a guy I loved for a little while and became obsessed with for a longer while. I was very young back then, but as idealist as I am today. How long after we break up with someone should we have that person in mind? What's the purpose of thinking about a person all over again?

We were colleagues at the university and had a brief love affair in the first year. After we broke up, I kept thinking about him. It was hard not to do so since our paths crossed on a daily basis. I kept looking for signs of his feelings towards me in everything he did, in his gestures, in his words, in his overall behavior. I was experiencing an outburst of imagination, which I translated into poetry. My frantic mental activity required a person to share my full palette of emotions with. And this is what friends are for. I had a best friend as a confidant. Someone to trust and feel at ease with when talking about love. Or obsession.

I think about love all the time. For artists, love equals inspiration. I find myself writing nostalgic texts when I need to release some pressure from my heart. I always tend to go back to the past when I write. With painting, it is different because if I let my hand go free, I can discover some unknown things. Writing can be painful, it fixes the weight of the words on a support, but painting is more dreamy. I don't care about perspective, technique, quality. If I wanted to obey rules, I wouldn't have turned to art. There is something heavy inside myself and something feathery. This is why I paint and write. This is nostalgia.

It was a hot summer day and I was hungover. As I was diving deeper inside my obsession, I started feeling as I was drifting away somewhere in the middle of the sea, with no direction to go. There were times when life seemed meaningless. I was constantly questioning and doubting my path in life. If I have a high capacity of endurance now, it originates in those times. I met him and we went to a park close to my house. I looked at his face, looking for familiar gestures, like those I used to see when I closed my eyes. He had been constantly on my mind for the past two years. But only then, I was to meet the real person that fueled my imagination. He could have kissed me, he could have grabbed my hand and time could have stopped for a second. There is always a gap between how we want things to be and how they are.

The difference between true love and obsession is reality. Our ability to distinguish between how a person really is and how our imagination wants that person to be is just a matter of psychological exercise. We always tend to give some imaginary traits of character to the persons we love, it is part of the way human interactions work. But only when we manage to break those illusions, we can eventually conclude: it was true love or it was just obsession.

We met on that day and walked a few steps together because I wanted to know how could he be dating my best friend. This is such a common tale that no one should be surprised about. I was waiting for an answer that never came. And as the man I thought I loved, when I was only obsessed with him started revealing his true self, I could see my distorted image of him breaking into pieces.

The day when he could have grabbed my hand, but he didn't, we sat down on a bench and looked at children playing. He told me about my giant ego and how I will see, one day I will get a job and lead a normal life, how this is a temporary adolescent-like crisis and as years fade away, I will remember vaguely about an artistic rebellion against life I once had. The day when he could have honestly told me why he is dating my best friend, he went on chit-chatting about meaningless things, giving unsolicited advices about how to live the best cliché. And nobody stopped to applaud the glorious break of an illusion.

And I understood back then, in that summer day, sitting on a bench in a park next to my house, that he cannot deal with me, that what people call mad is something they do not understand, that overpasses their capacities and that there are people who will try to cut off your wings because they cannot imagine themselves with wings. Years passed by and I did not change that much. I don't remember if I called him a coward or I just felt pity for myself. For how love is ultimately a solitary experience, how most of the passions are built on lies we tell to ourselves and how there are wounds that some people create and only other people can heal. But in order to make possible the healing, we need to contribute to it ourselves.

The guy I was obsessed with and my former best friend are now married. They also have a child.

Why do we need to experience pain and longing for a person, why do we need to have our heads filled with thoughts about someone that is no longer part of our present, as we find ourselves completely alone in our rooms? This case of self erotica, the exploration of oneself through art or whatever the means has ultimately a purpose: to learn love and compassion for ourselves, for the entire being.

Our expectations are made of hope and waiting. Our expectations are those stinging our hearts because pain reminds us we are alive. When we reach a certain level of emotion, we lose the consciousness of our body, we mix up with the air around us. As if to mingle with the air around us is the best type of silence we could have. Hope and waiting are made of silence. But us, humans, we are talkative beings and sometimes we need to kill our old expectations, just to be able to build new ones. As long as we live, we will be looking for people with whom silence disappears.

THE BREAK UP

When is the best time to break up with someone? When do we know we reached a point from where no come back is possible? What is the science of breakup?

The end of the relationship in which I struggled for seven years gave me a sense of numbness or maybe it was just relief. I was either becoming an insensitive monster or maybe my feelings were so worn out during the arguments we used to have. While he was packing his things I was lying on the couch reading the last chapter of 1001 nights. While he was still packing, I left the house and I went for a walk, I smoked an undefined number of cigarettes while walking the empty streets and saw the most amazing sunset. A mystical sunset I would call it, the whole sky was misty and gray, except for a line draped in gold at the end of the clouds. That line stands for tomorrow.

He came back to take some more things and I was sitting stoned on a chair in the hallway, still wearing his shirt. I tried to help him wrap his toothbrush in a plastic foil, but it just seemed too hard to do it in my stoned state. I burst out laughing. I thought about the incredible lightness of being. The joke.

But the end happened a long time before his departure.

There comes a time in every relationship, when something collapses. It is called the crisis. Some couples manage to overcome it, some do not. That's life.

Something collapsed inside of me the day when he grabbed my wrists and looked me in the eye with hatred, uttering some very cruel words: it's your fault, I am unhappy because of you. As the skin around my wrists was bruising, I started realizing my heart was bruised as well. I was subjected to emotional abuse. I was trapped.

There are people who would always try to change you, that would never be satisfied with the things you do for them, they will keep asking for more and more as if your kindness is an unlimited resource of energy that they think they have the right to be connected to forever. Realizing this means reaching the point of no return in a relationship. There should always be a balance between what we take and what we give when it comes to emotions.

Maybe I should have left myself when I understood this, but breaking up is never an easy thing to do.

So I kept staying inside that relationship, striking a warrior pose. I thought I had to defend my dignity. It is so hard to break up because when we let go of a person, we actually let go a part of ourselves. Good or bad, it is part of ourselves that walks out the door, never to come back again.

Breaking up is not just the moment of departure when we say this is my road and this is your road, they will never meet again, but a continuous process that lasts between the day we realize we are hurt and the day we can let go of that wound.

For me it was a long, painful struggle. I remember us both sitting next to each other on the living room sofa.

It was one of the days when we remained silent, moving around the house as if the other one did not exist, but always bumping into each other when grabbing a dish or opening a door. I remember imagining that if I close my right eye while sitting next to him, I can make him disappear. So I told him: I have magic powers. And he said: you're crazy. Thus, a silent afternoon transformed into a tempest. But I still cared for him. I liked the warm touch of him, of his skin and the way he hugged me when we went to sleep, no matter how bad we fought during the day. Maybe we are afraid to speak the definitive words of breakup because we are afraid we will not be able to reach the same level of intimacy with someone else. We are afraid of our bare naked souls and secretly doubt if we are worth loving.

I believe we could not be together because we were too different, I had an artist temper and he granted more value to common sense. But I still do not know for sure if erotica works on the rules of similarity or difference. The life we were trying to build was standing on moving ground.

I remember me dancing on a table at the seaside, the smell of sea, the nightly freedom and the table a bit shaky because it was standing on sand. He was trying to remove sand from his shoes. We did not know back then that we were trying to raise a life on sand. I remember when we went on holiday together and he went to buy cheap champagne at 4 am. in the morning from the train station in a small town in the mountains. I used to borrow his little phobias and sometimes even to fight them. I killed many bugs in our tent during a summer in which we traveled around Europe. I remember the many barbecues we had under the nut tree in his garden before we moved in together, the many bottles of wine we drank in summer evenings and how young we were when we met. His blue pajamas and the office bag he used to wear when he was going to work, while me, like all the bohemians, just went back to sleep.

And then I remember falling asleep on the sofa and the sparkle of hatred I saw in his eyes that was probably in my eyes also. I used to fall asleep in his car with my sunglasses on, hoping he will not notice, hiding from him the hatred that could have sparkled in my eyes as well. Him accusing me of being too dramatic, my head in the clouds and me threatening to never forgive him. But I do remember his dreams and what linked us, a certain distance from the world, but a very different distance.

The science of breakup can be summarized in only a few words: the break up process ends when the resentment ends, when we can say I forgave you as I forgave myself.

THE TRANSFORMING POWER OF LOVE

Is it possible to have a major psychological change in adult age? Is it possible to overpass one of strongest human fears, that is nevertheless very common: the fear of living? When the man I loved asked me this, I was living with another man. I had a stable job and I was leading a normal life, I was on the path that everybody expected me to be. Sometimes the hardest thing to distinguish is what we really want from life and what others expect us to do.

When I left my country with the man I did not love, but I was sharing a life with, my greatest pleasure was to retreat in my room and lead an imaginary existence while reading a novel. If I were to move somewhere, I wouldn't choose a country, I would rather choose a novel to move inside. But this story I am about the tell you is real. Somewhere on this planet, it did happen.

I left my country to continue my scientific research in a field I was working for years. But I was too scared to leave alone, so I left carrying heavy luggage: the weight of a dying relationship.

We rented a small apartment and every day after arrival, we kept on arguing about various subjects, such as: who should do the dishes, the existence of aliens, the most suitable day to clean the house or the meaning of our shared life. We could never agree on anything, our apartment resembled a battle field, as we went on breaking dishes and sending sharp gazes, heavy with hatred, to each other. We were two strangers stuck under the same roof, who had nothing in common, except for a fear, that is nevertheless so common: the fear of loneliness.

We lived close to the sea. Sometimes in the morning, a seagull used to knock on our window. We woke up, we had coffee and ceased the war for a while as I headed to work. When I was waiting for the bus, I sometimes thought about what else to expect from life. I was emotionally drained, far away from home and living with a man who was more an enemy than a partner to share dreams with. I thought I had nothing else to expect from life and then, I fell in love.

Love triangles are very common, almost as common as the fear of loneliness or the fear of living. They are an indication of split personalities between the need for stability and the excitement of the unknown, between what we are and what we could become. An indication of the gap between what we want ourselves and what others expect from us.

Never disregard the ability of life to surprise us. One day we might have nothing to live for and the next, there is something waiting for us around the corner. Us humans, we need something to believe in because otherwise we are just leaves blown by the wind. I do believe in love and its power to transform the way we see the world and ourselves as part of it.

I fell in love with a man whom I noticed in the bus stop. I was intrigued by the thickness of the book he was reading. I remember the intensity of the first gaze we exchanged. Maybe it is true that when we meet someone for the first time, time compresses and we can catch a small glimpse of the future. Day by day, we started talking more and more. As we were getting closer, I discovered a fascinating person, someone who took the time to listen to me, whose kind way of being brought me comfort, a man with whom time seemed to stand still. Opening up my heart towards him and revealing my true self came natural. He was a handsome man and sometimes I took pleasure in just looking at him, talking or just being. When we were in the same room, I had the impression nothing else mattered and this uplifting feeling will accompany me forever. But things were not that simple.

The happiest ten minutes of my life were those when I was half running, half floating to meet him and discuss the future of our relationship. I was so happy out of misunderstanding because I thought what hindered us from getting even closer was just a natural shyness that we both shared. But life is twisted and complicated and that afternoon when he told me our relationship will remain platonic, I had to struggle hard not to burst into tears. Platonic because he, just like myself, already had someone to share a life with. I already knew that but a loving heart always finds out ways to shut up the reason.

What I will always remember from that afternoon when we met and talked and an earthquake happened inside of me, is that his eyes changed colour: from light to deep blue. From the heights of the sky, I was falling fast into deep sea. My hands were trembling and as I was heading to the bus stop, I became aware I had a strange way of stumbling upon my feet. When we reach a certain level of emotion, we lose the consciousness of our body, we mix up with the air around.

After the discussion, I did not feel like going home. Home was a far place, not the claustrophobic place I was sharing with an enemy. I decided to go to the beach, to imagine what the sailors felt when willing to leave. After the sea it could be just another land, but maybe it's also the future. As I was standing there looking at the sunset, I remembered being at home, sitting on the balcony in the dark with bats flying around, looking at the glow of the river. I remembered waiting for the dawn in my room with the window wide open just to hear the morning birds sing. And there I was, sitting in the cold and staring at the North Sea sunset. I had to travel the world to arrive to this emotion. Real journeys happen inside of us. The extent of surprise that life can bring will always outdo the limits of imagination. We cannot use imagination to predict the future in an accurate way. I tried to imagine life six months from then. But surprisingly enough, there was no pain, but a sort of comfort as if time remained suspended.

Time was moving on and the platonic relationship was flourishing. As we were getting closer to each other, my desire for self expression increased. I started writing long texts which I handed him personally and one Saturday afternoon, after I came back from a trip to Berlin, I started painting. I was 26 years old and I had never thought I had a special talent for painting, my life had been linear until then, slowly building my scientific career. I started painting because the emotional outburst I was experiencing needed to unravel its tempest. As if all my life until then, a side of me was sleeping and then an earthquake came and the grounds I was standing on rearranged. Painting has the freedom of a dream, what you cannot say, you can paint. I did thirty paintings in one month and the day before he left, I gave him a painting and a hug. What I got in return was his bike.

The day when he left, I was looking outside the window of my office. I saw the seagulls aligned on the roof of the neighboring building. I was tired and afraid of a nervous breakdown. I could not sleep too well the previous night, I kept waking up in the middle of the night, it was dark outside and I was dreaming about taking the train in the wrong direction. I woke up with a terrible headache, I dressed up slowly and went to work. In the bus stop, I acknowledged I will never hear his footsteps approaching me. I had to get used to this. And I also had another thing to do: to learn how to ride the bike he gave me.

The same day, when I got home after a tiring day, in which I walked around almost absent minded, I tried the bike. I did not tell the man I lived with that I had a bike now, he did not notice almost anything about me anyway, only the paintings that grew as a spider web annoyed him, he told me he would have been ashamed if someone visited and saw the paintings. But no one came visiting anymore, not even my parents. I told myself that the day I will leave the house, I will sneak out like a quiet thief, with all the paintings in my luggage. Never to be back again. But that day, I was only a refugee on the living room couch and the most priceless thing I had was the bike that the man I loved gave me. If he were a modern centaur, half man, half bicycle, giving me his bike was like giving me half of him. This is why it was priceless.

I went outside the apartment, stepped down the stairs and unlocked the bike. I had a strong sentimental reason to learn how this mysterious machine they call a bike works. I got on the bike and noticed the height was perfect, I tried to keep the balance, but the bike seemed to be having its own will. Then, I tried to keep a line straight without putting the feet down, but the balance is a delicate thing, I never had this equilibrium, especially when it comes to emotions. A lady stopped and asked if I was okay, probably I looked drunk. It was not far from the truth, I felt my nerves tense and painful all day. I answered something about being clumsy. We are never too old to learn something. The lady went away on her own bike wishing me good luck.

Alone again. I have to do it, there is a secret power pulling me forward, the time suspension, the magic. As I get on the bike and look forward, I see the image of my grandfather trying to teach me how to ride a bike, the infinity of a childhood landscape, a summer day that survived in my memory. I start pedaling and I wake up at the end of the street. I have been floating until here, with the wind blowing from the back. It is magic. It is working. In one hour I managed to do what I could not do in a lifetime.

The encounter with him had a deep transforming effect on my personality. Sometimes without touching the physical self, you can touch better the soul. Because you can touch a lot of people who will never really know your soul.

The day when I found myself completely alone, I woke up with a pain in my chest. A physical pain, as if something was shrinking inside me and I was diving into a sea of numbness. Everything started aching when I realized that I lost my hope that the man who gave me the bike would come back. The life he chose did not include me as part of his present. It was time to move on and take a brave step into the future. I was alone all the time, while sharing the house with one and ardently thinking about the other. He will never come back, it was just meant to be like this, to meet and activate a power that was hidden inside myself.

Psychological change is possible even in adult age and true love is one of the powerful forces that can trigger it. The change of the path we take in life is possible if we are wise enough to listen to our true inner voice. I heard mine for the first time as I was struggling inside a love triangle, split between a dying relationship that resembled a battle field and a platonic one that was emotionally rewarding, but incomplete. My true inner voice told me to first learn to love myself, to explore my own emotional depth and find the patterns that could lead to dissatisfaction. I took a sabbatical year to dedicate myself to my passions, painting and writing. I took time to unify my being, to distinguish between what I want and what others expect me to do. For the first time, I chose my own path in life: a journey of self expression, in search of the only truth that is fully accessible to myself: my truth. And if people can tune in to this truth then maybe they will feel inspired to find their own truth.

Meanwhile I came back home and sometimes in the morning, as I have coffee and look outside the window, before I start my artist routine, I remember the seagull knocking at the window and the bus stop where life started changing for me.

LONELINESS IN THE DATING APPS ERA

How often did you find yourself alone in your room, hugging your knees, feeling the warmth of your own skin and asking yourself: why am I so lonely, is my youth going to waste, with whom could I share all the things passing through my mind and most of all, where could I find that person?

I lack patience, I do not know if it is only a psychological trait of mine or it is also the effect of the fast-forward culture we live in. And like all the impatient, lonely people, I am on Tinder. At night, wrapped up in blankets and velvet pyjamas, I find myself in the posture of a modern odalisque, swiping left or right and waiting for miracles to happen. Or at least something pleasant.

In the past year, I have been in touch with a chess grand master that turned on my sapiophile needs, an editor of a magazine that praised my poetic style, an incredibly handsome man that looked and acted like a Greek god, and a nomad that stopped his globe-trotting for a while to come meet me. I also had a date with an architect that almost made me lose my head. All these and I am still alone. Because in a fast moving world in which immediate satisfaction is easily graspable, people started forgetting the basic rules of erotica. The approach, the retreat, the longing, the looks, the desire to dissolve into the other person, the mental closeness. It is like a dance. I do not know if I am a good dancer, but some people just keep stepping on my feet. Erotica is a dance that requires warm up and practice. A lot of practice.

My encounter with the architect that almost made me lose my head lasted about one week, enough time to pass through all the stages of a relationship. This is love in the times of Tinder, this is ars amandi nowadays. But now really, is it?

I met him on a Sunday afternoon at the end of summer. It was so hot that the city seemed to be standing still. As I was slowly approaching, he waved at me and I had that strange impression of meeting an old friend, not someone for the first time in my life. We had a coffee at a terrace and introduced ourselves briefly in the same manner in which someone would stand up at a business meeting, saying: *I am Laura, I paint and I write, I am looking for a lover.* His name was John, he was an architect and he was looking for sex. But no one uttered these precise words, we just looked at each other, my gaze falling over the slight tremble of his hands, his eyes rolling over the tip of my long hair and my breasts.

How often did you ask this question: what do you want from me? How much more peaceful would you be today if you did? I sometimes dream about a world in which people talk honestly about the way they feel and what they want because all the unspoken words and the misunderstanding they imply are those turning against us in the form of depression, resentment and frustration.

I really liked him, I liked his curly hair, his broad smile and a certain shyness that is so appealing to people with excessive imagination. When he grasped my hand in the bus stop at the end of our date, I could already feel thousands of bubbles of champagne exploding in my head. Somebody stop me before I become too cheesy and start talking like Doctor Heart. Or Paolo Coelho on drugs. Later that night, we took another step into our fast-forward relationship. I found myself lying in bed and listening to his voice on the phone: what do you do right now, on which side are you lying, do you like it this way. You know, those things. Yeah baby, fuck me.

A few days later, the inevitable happened. But, dear God, what a pleasant inevitable! As my body was slowly abandoning, he kept whispering sweet nonsense into my oh-so-sensitive ears. I am not a masochist, I am a woman and like all women, I am a sucker for sweet words. If you say forever, I believe you.

And then, silence fell. Our fast-forward relationship was approaching the cold war times. No more how-are-yous, no more proposals, nothing. So after some days of self torture, I decided to speak up my mind and I sent him a message:

> I think people should not separate their emotional side from the physical side, they are strongly connected. I don't know what you wanted from me and I didn't get the chance to ask. I am a sensitive person and all my emotions build up inside. This is why I keep quiet sometimes and do not express my desires clearly. Now I am a bit upset because I was too impulsive and did not act in harmony with what I want. I really liked you and otherwise I wouldn't have tried to reach you. But there is nothing that I can do. I will just go on looking for people that share a similar philosophy about what being a whole person means.

I still do not know for sure if erotica works on the rules of similarity or difference. But what I do know is that those who find themselves questioning loneliness often are at the same time those who enjoy dancing the most. Try to leave a man and a woman alone in the same room for a while and see what happens. It is the same dance our parents did, standing at the roots of the great mystery that is life. People are born out of love and this is what keeps the world moving forward.

My name is Laura, I paint and I write. I am looking for a lover. I used to be on Tinder, swiping left or right while lying on my left side in bed in my room, wrapped up in warm blankets and velvet pyjamas. Maybe a lonely man reads my text and would like to meet me. I hope I expressed my intention clear enough. I will do my best not to step on your feet when we dance.

THE LUSTFUL IDEALISTS

There comes a time in the life of every woman when one deeply understands both the nuns and the lesbians. And there comes a time when she says enough, I am tired of this loneliness, I have the right to go crazy, I do not want to feel split anymore between my sensualist and my idealist nature, I want a lover, I want to go home in late autumn evenings and find warmth in the arms of a man, I want to stretch in bed and receive tender kisses on the back of my neck. Why do I sometimes feel guilty for receiving pleasure from a stranger, whose artists hands made me feel loved and adorned? It is not my fault that the man I loved the most could control himself so much that he never touched me. It is not my fault that the man I lived with caressed me with one arm and bruised my skin with the other. These all should belong to the past now. I have the right to go crazy, to find myself a lover from Mexico and travel the world together. I want love every night until I find satisfaction in fully abandoning myself. There comes a time in the life of every woman when she says: I had enough with so much logic, I want feeling. And feeling comes with a good friend: lust.

When I arrived in Lisbon, it was a clear, sunny spring morning. I wandered on the narrow streets and marveled at all the beautiful things that crossed my path: ripe oranges hanging in the branches of a tree next to an old cathedral, the deep blue reflections on the feathers of the peacocks living in the castle's yard, the sounds of fado coming from the windows of small cafés, carrying all the nostalgia of far away lands and missing lovers. I spent the days outside, walking up and down the hills and resting at the high viewpoints with a glass of orange juice in front of me. It was when I was devouring an octopus for dinner that I become aware of my loneliness. I am a young woman and I need a lover. And then, I found myself two lovers.

There are some very impatient people that hope all their issues will be solved straight away. They deposit their hopes in an hypothetical lover, in a life changing job or something as improbable as winning the lottery. But life is a journey, we travel through time, on real roads and on the inner paths. Instead of wishing for the impossible we could look straight away to the things within our immediate reach. It is up to your imagination to live well.

I am not a hypocrite, I am perfectly aware that applying in real life the psychological knowledge I have is not an easy task. But I try and I will keep trying all my life. If you happen to be an idealist in search of a cure for your own tail-biting process, you can keep calm, I can bring you solace. Your ideals will never come true, but this doesn't mean you should stop having them. Learn to live with them, accept them, just like accepting the fact that you spend a third of your life dreaming. When I was a child unsure of how lust matters work, I used to go to sleep telling myself: I should fall asleep fast and rest cause when I grow I will be busy all night. Adults, trading dreams for lust.

Jake was a sculptor and I met him while I was visiting the studio of a friend. I kept looking at his hands, I always liked an artist's touch. There was a magnetic force drawing me to him, he was a tall, handsome man, with delicate features and a calm way of being. I always liked handsome men. I am not shallow, I am an artist. Physical beauty is like a promise for the beauty within a person. Artists will always look for that beauty within, will try to catch it and bring it back to the world, saying: *it exists, beauty exists.*

When Jake introduced me to his friend, Richard, I was looking for a dancer for a performance of mine about fears. There are many fears we are subjected to, even if we are aware of this or not. The fear of loneliness is nevertheless so common. Fears usually come in pairs, fueling inner conflict. The fear of loneliness is opposed to the fear of love, the fear of letting go and becoming transparent to another person, the fear that you will eventually get hurt. But most of the fears are just in our head, it's ourselves against ourselves. Painting is a very good tool to raise consciousness and only after you are able to paint your fears, the words will come. And a fear you are able to say out loud is not that big of a dragon anymore.

Richard was a nomad, he kept traveling the world back and forth looking for the excitement of new experiences. He had a broad smile and a piercing gaze that made me feel a bit uncomfortable, as if he could see not only through my dress, but also the most intimate depths of my soul.

Later that night, we were all three sitting on the couch in Jake's studio. We kept having wine and talking. I was sitting in the middle, in one of my favorite yoga postures, my neck relaxed and staring at the electric fan on the ceiling. I was thinking this is something they have only in warm countries. It was when I remembered my first winter journey as a child that I felt warmth invading me. So here we are, we have Doctor Heart, the idealist, well-known for the words of wisdom, sharing a couch with two men and ready to unleash the animal sleeping inside. And Doctor Heart, the idealist, should confess: this scenario was not part of the mentioned ideals. But, dear God, it was pleasant.

Love bites on my breasts, on my neck and on my inner thighs.

When I woke up the next morning and while stretching and turning in bed, I started thinking about happiness. What is happiness? It is not a race to catch some well-set fantasies, but that moment when you stop to take a rest. I took a piece of paper and scribbled these words: *dress in pink, go to Puerto Rico, become an epicurean.*

When we moved in together, there were people who thought I have gone crazy. But they were the same people that thought I have gone crazy when I changed my path in life and started painting. When I took a brush in my hand for the first time, it was as if the gates of my inner world opened and I started letting visitors come inside. It is a complex inner world, one of deep anxieties, of unanswerable existential questions, but a world that contains within itself, the hopeful quality of struggle. There are people who think that when I abandoned my stable job for painting, something got inevitably broken inside my head, but I do know that only then it started getting fixed.

There are people who will try to cut off your wings

because they cannot imagine themselves with wings. Don't be quick to judge others. As long as they do not disturb you, people are free to fly wherever they please. Now, I don't say that everybody out there go for threesomes, just look inside your heart and see how much love you are capable of. And give yourself that love first.

THE BEST DATE YOU CAN HAVE IS WITH A THERAPIST

Love, even if it lasts one day or five years, it is still love. This is what the sex therapist told me. He said: look me in the eye, what's the matter with you, you are such a beautiful woman, why are you alone for so long. Wait a little, I want to know you better. Do you trust me? and shook my hand. I laugh and I say: now it's the psychologist talking. Can you really separate them, your professional life and your personal life? Can you disconnect your brain from your patients? Are we going to have a date or you will treat me like one of your patients?

I felt a bit uncomfortable as if he could see through all my protective layers, but he also triggered a desire of affection inside me. A warm heart calls for a warm heart.

He said: I treat borderline, anxiety, depression, everything. And sex issues. Sex is very important, I believe in Freud's theory, he went on speaking. I like Jung, it is a matter of psychological profile, I think. I like Jung because he allows a little space space for the unknown and spirituality. Sex is very important, indeed, but it is not everything, although there are times in the life of a person when it completely dominates the behavior of a person.

I still don't know if erotica works on the rules of similarity or of difference, but I am very stubborn about investigating this matter. Erotic issues are very important because they actually reflect the desire of people to connect to each other. And when I say erotic, I don't mean only sex, but all the other aspects of human interactions. Erotic issues are one of the biggest causes of prolonged pain. I deeply understand people's need for solace and relief from all their suffering, but there is no magic trick that can bring us instant gratification. This is why it is good to filter through our own thinking process everything that happens in this journey in quest for solace. Cause my solace might be different from yours.

You like Freud, I like Jung. You are a man, I am woman. You Tarzan, me Jane. It should work.

If I sleep with you or if I show you my innermost vulnerability, take it as a present. I am offering myself to you. Just be gentle and kind, I don't expect anything else. I don't understand those people who judge a woman for allowing the possibility of reaching a certain intimacy level from the early phases of a relationship. They call her a slut while looking from the outside, they judge and invoke the highest levels of morality, while having their minds filled with all kinds of dirty thoughts. You know what my problem is, dear sex therapist, I can see so well through people's intentions, I feel the complexity of their emotions and I am able to spot the contradictions in their speech. We are all good and bad at the same time and I know that the more judgmental and vocal our conscious attitude, the more instinctual our hidden side is. Relax, take it as it is. Be gentle. Be kind. Make love. And learn how to receive a present that someone gives you. And only then, our hearts will be able to communicate.

Intimacy means walking naked around the house without being fully aware that you are naked. Intimacy means receiving random kisses on my forehead or on my wrists. Intimacy means having the tip of my hair wet while lying in the bathtub together and you holding my legs so that we reach that delicate equilibrium that only people who dance on slippery surface together can reach. Intimacy means meeting your smile and your lustful gaze in the living room mirror. Intimacy also means the promise your body makes to me, that you won't hurt me and you will want to protect this vulnerability of mine because you find it beautiful, not silly. I can be so naive at times, but this naivety of mine is the same trait that hinders me from becoming bitter. I can be so mistrustful at other times, but this trait of mine is what hinders me from spreading around my emotional energy up to exhaustion. You see, my dear sex therapist, I am a complex person. Like all of us. I need love. Like all of us.

Intimacy also means being completely honest about your desires and intentions. And I can see all the kinky scenarios passing through your mind while reading this sentence. Intimacy is like the sweetest taste you find hidden deep inside a fruit. But before we reach that level of intimacy, tell me about you. Tell me who you are, my dear sex therapist. Tell me what life means to you, tell me your fantasies, while gently pulling my ear. Talk to me, my dear sex therapist cause I am a conversation animal and we are granted tongues to speak and lick each others fears like two cats pampering each other.

Tell me, my dear sex therapist, do you have a girlfriend? There are moments in our life when time stops for a second, we freeze and allow the sadness of past and future moments to invade us. Answers and questions that we already heard. Loneliness that we clearly foresee at a point in the future. That incredible sadness of things that already happened and we cannot change anymore. That incredible sadness of things to come that we cannot control. People hurting each other in a never ending weakness chain. Do you have a girlfriend? I do. So let us speak a little about cheating. And about sweet lies we all tell to protect the others. And about what's fair or not.

So we discuss whether people are polygamous by nature or not. It could be cause we all experienced attraction to another person while being in a relationship. If we put that attraction into practice, this is a totally different topic. There are many types of cheating, meaning being dishonest to a partner. But maybe the one that hurts us the most is the emotional infidelity. Because the full palette of emotions we experience includes pain. And being dishonest leads to emotional isolation and a sort of emotional war that happens inside ourselves. If you want to become polygamous, I find it fair enough, just make sure you send a notice to all the people involved.

I wonder if people prefer to be lied to and go on living in their bubble or would they rather hear the truth, no matter how painful that might be.

I will let you guess how my encounter with the sex therapist ended or maybe I will tell you another story about this some day. In Romanian, we have a saying: *don't do what the priest does, but what the priest says.* Priests, therapists, artists, we are all human indeed, with a lustful nature and a sparkle of divinity glowing every now and then. My solace might be different from yourself, so filter everything through your own thinking and feeling system. Don't expect anyone to illuminate you, but yourself. Trust yourself, be gentle and kind to your whole being and keep your heart open and honest enough to be able to learn from every experience. Much love from Doctor Heart, the woman who once dated a sex therapist.

THE MEN WHO COME BACK TOO LATE BECAUSE THEY DO NOT UNDERSTAND HOW THE HEART OF A WOMAN WORKS

I remember the first time I met him. We were both standing next to a bar. It was dark and crowded and our eyes met. I recognized the look in his eyes because it was in my eyes also. Something passionate and dark. A sort of an attraction to purity. No mid tones. Either this way or that way. A reckless approach to life we all must have had at least once, especially in our early youth. He bought me a drink and starting from that point, life was not the same anymore. Love transforms us, the deeper the love, the deeper the transformation.

I remember all the times we met and that particular night when we met next to the theater. It was slightly raining and we walked together, my arm holding his arm and him holding the umbrella. Our footsteps echoing in the same rhythm on the empty streets. I remember his sensitivity, his intelligence and that destructive power we shared: passion. I remember our talks and their intensity, how we could have done anything together, except for one thing: bow down in front of convenience.

And now years passed. I talk to him and he says: my wife, my child, my unhappiness. I took a normal path in life. I still love you. And my heart squeezes a bit. I remember his father, me eating biscuits with him for breakfast after a sleepless night. Him telling me all over again that my eyes remind him of Catherine Deneuve and that I should not bow down in front of life. You are stronger than this coward that is my son, he says. We laugh and eat another biscuit. Two generations of bohemians sitting in the same kitchen.

And now he says: I have a son. I still love you.

I remember the day when we drank cheap cognac in a bar next to the train station and me carrying a constant fear in my chest. I was very close to disintegration once, this is why I can endure many things now. I remember a certain morning. The window was open and I could hear the birds. I always liked to wait for the dawn. For those birds only. He caressed my arms for hours and maybe then he understood that what I need is tenderness, not passion. I wonder if it was the last time I saw him. My memory became foggy.

There are people who will always think you remained at the age they last saw you. I am 28 now. And I tell him: there are times when I feel alone, but it's better like this, I have freedom. I might end up an old lady with many cats, but I like cats anyway and I did too many compromises in life, I am doing none. He says: go on living your legend. But don't get married, when you will be old and tired of too many experiences, I will ask you to marry me.

My heart squeezes, I think about his father and his son and my passionate way of being. All I could say is this: I do care for you and always will, but if my passion burnt down, I do not come back. Think about here and now, it's everything that matters. I trust my destiny and life made us meet again so that I could tell you this: I found light and I have hope. And if you look inside yourself, you might find it also.

All the men in my life ended up coming back to me at some point, but what surprises me and saddens me at the same time is that they all ended up coming back too late. My artwork is orientated on emotions. Writing about how I feel is a feminine approach to understanding life. But we all have feelings, don't we? I am sure there are many women out there resonating with my words, but reading my stories might be interesting for men as well in order to get an insight of the way women psychology works. I believe men and women should be equal in rights and opportunities, but we are fundamentally different in the way we behave or react. We are not supposed to lead wars against each other, but to complete each other.

This is a story about men who came back too late because they did not understand how a woman's heart work.

There are ten thousand ways to fight bitterness and ten thousand ways to avoid resentment and frustration, but then, there are words that should reach the person they are meant for. It might come easy to withdraw inside oneself and get covered in numerous protective layers of dignity. If your ego bleeds and you won't let your wounds speak, you will eventually drown. All the unspoken words are like arrows that come back to us and sting our hearts. It is human to feel hurt and it is human as well to speak about this. Broken communication leads to a broken heart. A broken heart can be healed of course, the heart is a delicate mechanism, I think about those anatomical diagrams–blue coming in and red coming out. Blue because the blood carries oxygen and we all know that life is about breathing. I believe all the illnesses are a consequence of unbalance and that includes of course, heartaches.

Where were you when I needed you? What were you doing all the times when I called for you and my voice echoed in the desert? And why do men always think that when they decide to come back, they find the same person they abandoned? Imagine you are looking at a tree, at all the beautiful ocher shades of its autumn leaves. And then imagine you turn away for a little while and when your eyes come back to look at the tree, there is nothing there anymore. Meanwhile, the wood of the tree transformed into a book. And everything that was there for you to see, will just belong to the memory from now on. Our memory is a space so translucent and feathery. But still so vivid because all the things that existed at some point go on existing in that other life we could have lived, but we didn't.

All the waiting in vain in those times when my heart was still open. All the questions, the doubts, the loneliness. The hope. If you do love me, why don't you tell me? Because otherwise I will just end believing that you really don't. As long as you still have the capacity to trigger an emotion inside me, there is the possibility that I might come back to a love affair that belongs to the past. But if you decide to come back after I already managed to put structure inside my emotions, it might be too late. I make my decisions based on how a certain situation would make me feel and that is what makes us, men and women be different. If the day when you decide to come back, the only emotion I have left is the potential feeling of unease, as if going back to the past would be just an extra weight put around my neck, given all the emotions I passed through during your absence, be sure I will not come back. It would not be revenge or cruelty, but just the realization of the fact that life can go on without you in the same way it already did.

I broke up with my ex-boyfriend when I was truly convinced there was nothing left there, when I realised the balance will always be inclined towards sadness and frustration with him. It was when I understood I do not deserve all that unhappiness that I was able to step away telling myself: I tried enough, may life be kind to me from now on.

After some time, he tried to reach me again. He said we should get back together because we will never manage to know someone else as well as we knew each other. He claimed he regretted everything, but I could not forget the bruises on my wrists and on my heart. When I told him to fuck off for the last time, it was the night when he sent me a poem about dreams of murder. He said what's the matter dear, don't you know E.E. Cummings? And then I knew: I was afraid, I feared him as I feared myself, I wish I never wasted my years, hiding from him in the same room. The night when I told him to fuck off for the last time, I had been having wine and smoking, floating for a few days, as if living inside a poetry about dreams of killing time. I said what's the matter dear, don't you know myself, I always mean when I say something. I used to be afraid, but I am not anymore. The night when I told him to fuck off for the last time, he said I'm sorry and I said I don't care, I met someone. He called me cruel. And I don't even like poems about dreams of murder.

ALL THE WOMEN WHO WAITED FOR THEIR LOVERS TO COME BACK

All the times I waited for you, sitting on a bench in a park, looking at the pigeons or sitting alone in a café, looking outside the window, watching the passersby laughing or frowning as if looking at the flow of a river. All the times I waited for a smile, a sign to break the silence or a letter of yours letting me know you do care. All the times I tried to decode your silence as if it were the greatest mystery of the universe. All the times I waited for you inside the dark room of a theater, half asleep in my velvet chair, waiting for you as if waiting for Godot.

You never know where silence went, if silence installed inside your chest or inside your heel, if it can be healed or not.

And then I got up, the bench remained empty behind me. There was a bit of cold coffee on the bottom of a cup. The wind softly blew the curtains of an empty café. And I walked around, with the fresh memory of a theater play I watched that just made my torment more vivid. I walked the empty streets of my hometown, not knowing where home is anymore because it's been two years now since I live in a bubble.

I arrive home and I sit in the kitchen, I am still waiting

for my hunger to stop, I look at the birds I painted last night and I invoke all the gods of structure to come back and put structure into my thoughts cause I am drifting somewhere far away from you and far away from myself. I will wait here in the kitchen, hoping for my hunger for you to stop, while deep frying in oil color a bird of paradise.

Another day passes and I am still bathing in silence as if swimming on the bottom of the ocean. I think about all the women that waited for their men to come back, lovers who left on journeys on the sea or to war. Some did come back and some didn't. That's life. You didn't leave on a ship or to fight in the desert, you just left to battle yourself. And that is the contemporary war we are all leading. Ourselves against ourselves.

You still didn't come back and the heart is a delicate mechanism, I think about those anatomical diagrams, blue coming in and red coming out. Blue because the blood carries oxygen and we all know life is about breathing. I look at an X-ray of my heart today and it is all blurred, I see all kinds of birds and fish dancing around. I must have gone mad with all this waiting. Cause madness is an easy way to escape pain. But I am a warrior myself, I lead the same private wars everyone else is leading. Ourselves against ourselves, in an heroic quest to fight loneliness and distance. I will not go mad, I will just go swimming every now and then on the bottom of the ocean, among colorful jellyfish and dancing corals. And those seahorses I like so much. I believe madness is just an immense sadness we do not understand.

I am still waiting for you to come back because I am an incurable romantic, although being romantic is not disease. But with time, my waiting changed in tone and color, it became more abstract. I started learning how to live with it. Despair changed to hope and as time passes, it will start changing into something similar to a religious feeling. Cause my religion is passion and my expectations sky high. There is much love inside my heart and I do not want to kill it. Love is a pure, uplifting feeling, that has nothing to do with possession. This is why people who are capable of much love start becoming spiritual at some point in their life.

I don't go that often to the cafés alone, I laugh and frown like everybody else. But somewhere inside that delicate mechanism that is this heart of mine, there will always be a place that is only yours.

I still don't know if you will ever come back or not, but what I do know is that this waiting is worthy, cause when I cease the war against myself for a second and I stop to look around, as if looking at the other spectators during the break of a theater play, let's say for instance 'Waiting for Godot', I see myself in the mirror with a bigger heart now. It must be filled with red birds and blue fish and hope and longing. And love, of course.

THE POETIC MOOD

I woke up with this mood today. It's cold and raining, just like in late November, although it's still August. It's almost a year now since I came back home and I don't know anything about the future. I am still sensitive to rain, those years spent in the Netherlands left a mark on my heart. But now, as time passes, it seems to me as if I dreamt about it. The only true rain is the one I feel today on my skin.

I remembered all the times I walked empty streets, in foreign or familiar places with something trembling inside my chest. I walked around the city trying to catch the mood, to put it into words, as if trying to catch a rare bird and express the tenderness it lights inside your heart. It is a tender feeling the one I have today.

I am human, I have feelings, therefore a rare bird exists. And it trembles inside my chest as I go on walking, as the wind goes on blowing, the rain goes pouring and I go out seeking company.

There is a dim light inside the café, I look outside the window, the wind blows the curtains. It's one of those days when I just feel like looking outside the window. I must have done it many times in a dream. It was a window facing a forever gray sky with seagulls flying in circle all the time. The window was close to sea, but it was so thick I couldn't hear anything.

That bird is still inside my chest, but I make it quiet for a while, I start drinking wine and we play monopoly. So serious as only the people that have birds in their chest that need to be quiet for a while could play. We laugh. And the memory of rain vanishes like one of those dream that one forgets.

There are novels in which it rains for half of the book. I know one written by Jose Saramago. There are novels in which the main characters spend their loneliness in an almost voluptuous way, they go to work, they come back home, they cook dinner, eat alone and maybe look outside the window. I know some written by Haruki Murakami. But good novels tell a true story. I am a poet and I believe poetry is a way of being. I am specialized in moving something inside people's heart.

I don't want to be alone anymore. That is all my trembling heart was trying to tell me. And now that the bird has a name, I can open the window and let it fly away.

If I were to write a poem now, I would write only this: *Be gentle to the birds of tenderness.*

I BET YOU WANT TO BE HAPPY

I bet you are unhappy trying to pretend you are tough, trying to pretend you don't care. Because you don't know where you learnt that being emotional is a weakness. Hiding all the time. Maybe you learnt this at school or maybe just life taught you this: we live in a world based on action. Make decisions, write down your future, plan. Hide your tears when they come. But no one taught you how to handle a flood. You retreat further down inside yourself, drifting on the irrationality you gained. You are a prisoner of yourself. You must have denied your true nature for a long time now. There is a door in front of yourself, but just like in a dream, it is constantly moving. You look for the key to open that door, but your pockets are empty. And you don't know who has that key, if you had it and lost it, if you ever really had it or if someone else stole it from you.

Who has the key for my happiness? Who stole it from me? Where am I? Where can I learn how to create a key?

Be your own teacher. Know yourself. And if you really like planning, consider attending these special classes where you can learn something about yourself. About what you really want because no one else can teach you that. Write a note and post it on that constantly moving door. And be patient.

I bet you are unhappy, woman, hiding some of your most beautiful gifts: your vulnerability and your need for protection. I understand you are afraid because what was first a fear became a monster. And the name of that monster we all fear is loneliness. We cannot do everything by ourselves. There are nights when you just want to put your head to rest and feel someone's hands running through your hair. Late November nights, when you gain an almost painful consciousness of the warmth of your body dissipating in solitude.

I bet you are unhappy when your woman closes her ears in front of your logic. You see her refusing to think about something and drifting further away from you in silence. At some point there must have been a wound that no one spoke about. No one cried for. I bet you feel like drifting away in your own solitude when she disregards your desire for action. When she leaves you outside her world and closes all the doors and windows and you see her eyes getting darker and a sadness glowing inside them that you do not understand. And you are too afraid of the unknown like all of us. You see her diving inside a sadness that is a bit mysterious and a bit foolish at the same time. And it saddens you as well because she stands behind a door where you cannot enter and make her laugh. That bright laughter you remember so well because you did want to make her happy. And now you are both flooded and no one taught you how to deal with a flood you do not understand.

But I bet you want to be happy.

Let's meet somewhere in between. I will be standing in front of that constantly moving door I told you about and you will be standing in front of your door. I bet you will be a little afraid and I will be as well. But when we will open our own doors, maybe we will meet each other and find out with surprise it was only one door. And fresh air will start running between our two worlds. And we will be happy. The end.

I bet you think I am an incurable romantic while reading this, but being romantic is not a disease. It was a romantic impulse to write these two words: the end. But that is not the end, the world goes on running, men and women go on dating, living, loving, sometimes even going to war against each other. And ultimately we die. I am chameleon, but unlike a classical chameleon, I display high adaptability not to the outside world, but to the inside world. A reservoir of dreams and emotions, which are not only mine, but they sleep inside the depths of the human soul. We might think sometimes that we are hopelessly isolated inside ourselves, until we find out with surprise there are people passing through similar situation. We are never really alone. Trust me, I am Don Quijote, the chameleon.

A LETTER TO ONE OF MY FAVORITE WRITERS

Dear Henry Miller,

To paint is to love again, indeed. There were times in your life when you just closed yourself in your room and painted like crazy for days. You didn't care about anything else but your watercolors because you loved life so deeply and that was the best way you found to express your love. To paint is to love again and the hardest thing to do is to replicate the drawing of a child, you said. You wanted innocence and freedom and love and these are great lessons for all of us to learn.

A writer that paints is actually more common than people might think. Sylvia Plath had a major in art and literature. John Fowles had an eye for beauty and wrote expressive descriptions in his journals of the landscapes that touched his artistic sensitivity, he was especially fond of the purity of light and color typical to the Greek islands. The time spent in Spetses as an English teacher inspired him to write *The Magus*. In one of his journal entries, he talks about a lack of balance between the quantity of art people consume and the amount they produce. He goes on, pointing out that the mentioned unbalance could lead to what he called "the constipation of the demiurges." How beautiful and funny at the same time! I am sure you would have liked it. Even Victor Hugo did them both. I believe it is wrong to limit ourselves to only mean of expression, when creativity comes, we should just bow down in front of it.

I think about love all the time. For artists, love equals inspiration. I find myself writing nostalgic texts when I need to release some pressure from my heart. I always tend to go back to the past when I write. With painting, it is different because if I let my hand go free, I can discover some unknown things. Writing can be painful, it fixes the weight of the words on a support, but painting is more dreamy. I don't care about perspective, technique, quality. If I wanted to obey rules, I wouldn't have turned to art. There is something heavy inside myself and something feathery. This is why I paint and write. This is nostalgia.

I am a passionate reader, I have been reading constantly since I was a child. My room is filled with paper books. They say you can live a multitude of lives through reading. Your books, Henry, have a special place in my collection. When I like a writer a lot, I just go and buy all his books and sometimes I get sad if that writer died and I know he cannot write more books anymore for me to devour. I have the whole collection of Haruki Murakami, Isabel Allende, Jose Saramago, Gabriel Garcia Marques and Antonio Tabucchi. And of course, your books, Henry, standing next to another book that fascinates me, Codex Seraphinianus of Luigi Serafini, an illustrated atlas of imaginary beings, that required the invention of a whole language and even an alphabet that goes with it.

I walked with you the streets of New York or Paris and followed the solitary pace of your thoughts while wandering through the forests of Big Sur, California. I also go for a walk every evening to clear my head and meditate about the meaning of all the things we live. I always looked for meaning in the books I read and in the encounters with people that crossed my path in life. We walk around, apparently with no purpose, but it's up to us to filter from the multitude of emotions and experiences what is life really about. I am not worried I might have not found an answer yet to the many existential questions that blossomed in my head and I then address to God, to Jung or to you, Henry. You were 88 years old when you died and you wrote somewhere that those who had moments of great despair are those who are also aware of how great the instinct to live is. These might not be your precise words, but I know what you mean: when someone constantly thinks about death but finds himself running from the bus that could crash into him.

To paint is to love again, you said, and you did love for many times in your life, with the pure heart of a never grown up. It is a matter of purity to be able to fall in love again despite the pain that inevitably comes with it. All the letters you wrote are proofs of your passion: the passionate letters you wrote to Anais Nin and to the women that were your lovers. You did write many letters in your life, addressed to writer friends, such as Lawrence Durrell, or just to people that wrote you from all over the world when your inner voice started resonating inside people hearts. You said in those times you wouldn't do anything else all day, just respond to letters, sometimes you even forgot to eat. I understand you well cause since people discovered my writing, I sometimes forget to eat as well. People need solace and if I just happened to have the gift to put emotions into words, I should use it wisely. There is so much healing power in words.

I traveled with you across Greece and across America and I marveled at the wisdom of the traveler, that had an eye for the beauty of the lands and an eye for the people inhabiting them. You were quite adventurous and last but not least, I should tell you I really enjoyed reading your lustful adventures. Lust is part of the human nature, I believe it should not dominate our entire behavior, but we shouldn't also remain deaf to nature's call.

Love comes with lust. Painting comes with love. Writing and painting go well together. And this is a love letter for all those people who know how to enjoy life. To paint is to love again, you said, and I would just add: to love is to live. And your sincere writing, dear Henry Miller, has touched me deeply.

Love,
Laura

THE BOHEMIANS

I was born in a year with heavy snowfall, that just happened to be the year of the Cernobil accident. I was barely two weeks old when I abandoned the cat I was sharing a bed with to start my first winter journey, crossing the Carpatians with my parents. I kept travelling all throughout my childhood on a parents-propelled wooden sledge. I am a nomad at heart, I kept travelling all throughout my life to a million places, in my room, with my eyes closed. I remember the first flying lesson I took, while holding my father's right hand and my mother's left hand, me lifting my legs from the ground and allowing the magic of imponderability to happen.

I never really lost that sense of magic, although there were times in my life I had the impression I failed miserably. I had this impression the most when it came to love matters.

In south France, after you cross the Alps, the vegetation starts changing and all those beautiful, colorful Mediterranean plants start appearing, you can catch the glimpse of the sea for the first time. In the same area, there is a prison and it impressed me deeply when I noticed it for the first time because it perfectly mirrors a paradox: a prison close to the sea is like loving the wrong person. You feel the desire for freedom and you are trapped. I am a nomad at heart who sometimes chose the wrong companions.

Life with a bohemian is hard. There will always be a pile of books on the floor and you will stumble upon it on your way to the bathroom. The bohemian will start screaming at you: do not destroy the treasure, please don't leave any footprint on some Garcia Marques novel. And then, the bohemian will declare, with so much hope in her voice that if she finds a person madder than herself that will actually buy one of her paintings for the outrageous price that she fixed she will buy a plane ticket for Peru or Chile. To get off the plane, dressed in something that resembles a puma costume, straight into a novel by Isabel Allende or Mario Vargas Llosa, to climb the Andes and to cross the Amazonian jungle. The bohemian always wanted to move inside a novel. To try out some magic herbs if possible and forget entirely that it is physically impossible to move inside a novel. She will invite you to join this adventure. The bohemian will say all this while rolling a cigarette and will postpone again that very annoying action called dish washing, so mundane for an artist soul. The worms will eat us if we live according to your artist soul. But the worms will eat us anyway, cause living with a bohemian is not easy, the bohemian will tell you straight in the face the essential things: that we all grow old and that you might want to make love even when you will be all wrinkled, no matter how disgusting this may sound now. It's not easy to live with an artist, cause one morning, you might wake up being a character in a novel. And you might want to kill her because all the intimacy is gone with the wind. It used to be better when the bohemian woke up with different ideas, such as setting up an art colony or a philosophical and psychological society, everything at the same time because the universal man Leonardo da Vinci was born again and you have no idea how great an ego is sleeping in the same house as you. She will laugh at this last sentence so hard and there will be times when you will look at her astonished, not knowing if she is serious or not. You will sometimes wonder if you are sharing the house with a woman or just a naughty child. And one day, the bohemian will start painting and her art will multiply so fast, invading the house like a spider web. She will paint in oil, even cooking oil when she runs out of art supplies, she will mould the clay with the spoon you use for soup and you will be afraid like hell of those little creatures because maybe now the madwoman took up voodoo. She will paint restlessly so that she can stare at them for hours, standing still in silence, a silence that she kicked you out from when she closed her right eye. Because one day the bohemian discovered while sitting on the couch that if she closes the right eye, she can make you vanish, she has magic powers. She will occupy the living room table with brushes and many kinds of tubes, that will stain everything, including the artist's dresses. She will walk around wearing some turquoise blue at her wrist and yellow stains on her dress and you will know that she acts like this because she is in love. And you will know this because you know that look on her face when she is in love. And one day, the bohemian will put on a hat and will walk around the streets with no purpose, trying to understand the mysteries of the universe in your absence. All art is done during an absence.

I cannot see you too well, you are riding a white bike, you smile, you look happy, but the image is unclear, you say it is because of the speed. You like speed, but sometimes life runs so fast in front of our eyes, you are afraid we will forget everything, even the faces of our parents. This is why you ride so fast, you want to catch the truth before an unclear image gets imprinted in the memory. There is a secondary road on your right, the path becomes blurry because of the old oak trees. We are in the forest that surrounds the Kroller-Muller museum, the green gem of the Netherlands, according to the leaflet you read and then you put indifferently in your pocket. You try to keep a straight line while riding the bike, you seem to be very focused. It must be because you have learnt how to ride a bike recently, although you are 27. You scare an old lady when you are about to bump into her. But you don't seem to notice, you smile and fix one of your bags on the shoulder. You always wear two bags, filled with all kinds of useless thing, you say you want to be prepared, just in case. It's raining heavily, but you don't seem to notice, you pedal faster in the open spaces of the forest.

I need to hurry, in this country everything closes at 5. I want to see that painting of Van Gogh, Café terrace at night. I know all its details because I printed a picture of it and stared at it for hours. At home, I sometimes look outside the window, I like watching the speed of the clouds and the silent screams of the seagulls. I live close to the sea.

It's raining heavily but I don't care too much about that, I could pull the sunglasses from my bag. At least I can avoid water getting into my eyes. The locals don't seem to get wet, they don't seem to care about rain or water, I sometimes see them going out of the house with their hair wet after taking a shower. My grandma would go crazy if she heard that, she would say it's a sure way to die of meningitis.

We arrive at the museum and you run like crazy to the entrance. You say you need to see a painting. There was a time when I used to like Van Gogh as well, but then I don't remember what happened, maybe I just got isolated inside my own sadness. I remember all the art albums you used to give me as a present for Christmas or that one time when you bought me the letters of Van Gogh to his brother, Theo, for my birthday. I miss the way you used to be before you got isolated in your own sadness. I don't feel like entering inside the museum, so I just wait for you outside, smoking a cigarette. All paintings started annoying me since you started painting and they spread around the house like a spider web. I think you started painting because you are in love, but it's been a while now since you stopped telling me anything. You didn't even tell that you have a bike now, you just showed up one day riding that bike that I noticed at the entrance of our house and wondered whose is it. There are four apartments in the house. In one of them two beautiful girls live. In another one, there is a man living, who comes home drunk every evening, carrying a bag from McDonalds. Sometimes I hear him sing in his apartment, things like: I go to Spain or I am so tidy. And then, there is the girl that once knocked at our door to keep it quiet while we are loudly arguing.

You come back to the entrance of the museum, you seem nervous, you say: I couldn't see anything properly. We leave because it is getting dark and there are about five kilometres to pedal through the forest. You pedal slowly and sometimes I stop and wait for you or let you go ahead. There is no one else on the path we took, the forest is big and there are numerous routes to take.

I stop under a tree to smoke a cigarette, I see you passing by and smiling when you disappear around the corner. And then I hear a bump and a metallic sound on the asphalt. I knew you fell, but I just stay there for a little while in silence before I reach you. There is blood on your knees and tears in your eyes. I look at you and you say it hurts. Everything hurts.

I fell and I cannot help crying. But it wasn't just the physical pain because that one is sometimes easier to handle. I cry because just like in this forest, there are many roads we can take in life and sometimes we walk on these roads alone or other times accompanied. I cry because we can never really stop this journey, the moments that we freeze are just in our memory. And I a nomad.

I have a nomad soul, I wish to travel the world, so, eyes closed, I arrive in Siberia and look straight to the horizon. An insatiable look. Up lately, I dreamt about Creta and Bali. Islands in the sun. I remember the story about my grandmother's ancestors. Some tall, distant people, carrying the nostalgia of the Mongolian steppe in their eyes. A clear horizon is freedom.

I am one of those passionate people, who have a natural sense of drama and enjoyment of life. When I die, I want to look back and be able to say: *oh God, I did live.* All the years of living at high emotional intensity did not diminish my capacity to wish. I enjoy some good wine and good company. And laughters until the morning, when normal people go to work, and us, the bohemians, warm up our skins at the first rays of sun of a new day. Wake up at 12, paint, write and disregard the natural flow of life. I never grew up and settling down is like taking away the horse from a Mongolian passionate about clear horizons. As years go by, I understand the bohemians remain a few to choose from. I wish for a companion in life, someone with an adventurous spirit, maybe a nomad that still has the capacity to marvel in front of the beauties of the world. I get bored at writers' gatherings, a bunch of frightened people that recreate life from the intimacy of their rooms. I enjoy sharing, but a passionate way of sharing and I would sacrifice the delight of recreating life through writing for a real experience. Because there is fire burning inside me and no matter how many times life betrays me, I go on walking. Go on wishing. I never really lost that sense of magic.

TOURIST AT HOME

UNDERSTANDING PERSPECTIVE

I don't know how many rooms I have
Or how many souls*
I left my rooms in Leiden
And the room in Bucharest
I brought my soul home to Sibiu
To paint in my childhood room
like an actor that never left the stage in Sibiu
Like more actors that never left the stage
There
In my mirror
I see a girl painting clouds
On small pieces of soul
And trying to understand perspective
For artists
There is a mirror inside her painting
While I write all this
Some clouds entered my room
I am repeating these lines
I do my rehearsal while standing in front of the mirror
While standing inside the mirror
I go on painting
As I understand perspective
From the inside of the clouds

From the inside of my rooms.
I leave the room from the inside of my painting
Cause it's high time I start painting clouds
There should be a door in my painting with the mirror
So I can go on entering my souls.

The first two lines are a reference to one of the poems of Fernando Pessoa

BIRTHDAY STORIES

I was three years old
And coming back from the kindergarten with my mother
My birthday happened to be during the revolution
But I wouldn't care less
I kept insisting about a party.
I am passionate about many things
But my greatest passion is a question:
Why?
How can I explain to you what the revolution means
Or what are the stray dogs
Or what walking in Rahova means.
Years later, when the people were remembering the revolution
I was walking in Rahova
For my birthday
Sending love to the world
To the nomads
Remembering my passions.
Rahova is just a place
Just like the plane between Barcelona and Amsterdam
Is just a place in my birth times memory.
I am a time traveler
Passionate about doors and questions

Doors to the past, to the future
I hold a key and a magic power
That is my favorite question:
Why?
This year for my birthday
I received a stray dog as a present
I kept asking for it
While waiting for the party
Like a three years old
In times of revolution.
I kept sending love to the world from Rahova
But how can I explain to you what Rahova is?
I bought myself a dress
To splash it with color
Cause besides doors and a question I am passionate about this
Just splashing color on the world
Like sending love from Rahova
Or wishing in times of revolution.
The brightness high and the miserable downfall
Like a door to the past, one to the future
Linked by my favorite question
Why?
I came back and my new stray dog was gone
Before even possessing him
How cruel
Something taken away from you that is not really yours.
While splashing my dress with color
I had two distinct visions
One to the past
One to the future
But how can I explain this to you
A dark hallway with many doors

A shadow rushing towards one of them
Slamming the door and locking it
I don't remember which door the shadow entered.
And another one with a dark hallway
A shadow rushing out from one of the doors
And not remembering which door the shadow comes from.
I hold a key and a magic power
To passionately slam doors
Inside out.
Even if the doors are not really mine.
I don't own a stray dog, but a question:
Why?
People died or had birthdays during the revolution
They gave birth to wishes and questions
Magic powers and guns
Such as mastering or triggering
Emotion.

WHITE MAGNOLIAS AND MADNESS

I was walking around
And I met this lady
Wearing a mad glow on her beautiful face
I knew I met her before
In my dream about the lady with the white mask
How strange
The way everything links together
The numerous associations we do in our head
Some invisible currents
Carrying light from one place to another
It sometimes happen so fast
That if you don't take the time to explain how everything is connected
You will appear mad
I have always been very fast
Just like one of those invisible currents in my head
I could be a current myself
Carrying the light of my thoughts from one place to another.
So, one evening
While I was carrying my thoughts on the streets
I met this beautiful mad lady that I met before
In a dream

She was carrying two giant white bags
And selling white magnolias
In Bucharest
In February
How strange
I kept wandering on the streets
And I arrived in a park
There, next to a tree, just like in a botanical garden
It was written:
Magnolia.
And then I understood
The past is a flower
And images are stronger than words
In madness
And this is what madness is about
Selling magnolias in Bucharest in February
Without telling where you got them from.
So I went back home
Following those bright paths
Walking around the streets enlightened
Just like some invisible currents travel my head
And I started writing down
What that beautiful mad lady was carrying in her white bags
One bag of white magnolias for the past
And one for the future
Cause words are like flowers
And words can be stronger then images only if they describe them.

ALICE PRACTICING YOGA

Yesterday morning at breakfast
I realized there are people I might never see again
Or I might, but not as I thought
It might happen only
In another life.
And the very same day
I fell
I slipped on ice
But surprisingly enough I did not get hurt
I found myself in a yoga pose
On thin ice, at night.
It was neither sun greeting, nor child pose
But something in between
Like a cat granted those nine lives
Arching her back in cobra
Or like that Phoenix bird I once painted.
But my knee was there,
Triggering signals of that obsession.
I could tell everyday on a scale from 1 to 10 how much it hurts
Because I once said
If I were a pain I would paint the healing.
Hours later, I found myself

In a living room
Looking like Alice
With my detective costume and my hat
Sipping coffee from a cup
A drunkard pose
Which was neither sun greeting, nor child pose
I took to yoga to balance my mind
While looking for safety.
So I took a taxi to bring me to a safe place
Such as home
Where to practice my poses while asleep
Especially the Alice pose
In wonderland
Where on top of my head there is a hat
Which does not fit anywhere.
I took a taxi
And Bucharest
This city of soul aches
Was looking like a foreign city
I kept looking outside
Looking for ice to practice my poses
Thinking about all the troubles of a generation
I am part of
But still outside
Like Alice with her hands and legs outside the house
A pose of a never grown up
That lost the train of her generation
That wishes for warmth, but still keeps distance
Alice that would borrow children to show up at that reunion
Ten years after high school
Instead of settling down
She looks for the dawn

From the window of a taxi
Thinking about yoga and obsessions and future
And art that is sufficient to show it to only one person
Instead of showing off to the world.
The taxi slowly rolling on a street in Bucharest named Mântuleasa
That has something to do with a sacred geography
And religion
And even yoga
Just like the apartment on top of mine in my home town
An apartment inhabited by painters
Has something to do with a sacred geography
But I was too ashamed to knock at their door
And say
You might remember my child pose
But I came back as a loner
In adult age
Painting loneliness and the process of healing
Let me introduce myself
I am Alice
I do not fit anywhere.
It has something to do with a sacred geography
But in a way that is very hard to explain to a foreigner
In the very same way that is very hard to explain
The House of the People in fog
What are the Romanian people
And the aches of this generation
That produced Alices
That keep producing artwork
Because they once said
If I were a pain,
I would paint the healing.
After I wrote all these,

I could not sleep
So I smoked a cigarette at dawn
And I buried it in the soil meant for plants
May ash grow from this
And may I be granted rebirth
Like any Phoenix bird stuck in the body of Alice practicing yoga.

NEW YEAR'S MOOD

I was standing in the kitchen
Minus 17 outside
Wondering what's the temperature of my heart today.
Since I started recording my moods
In paintings and poems
Everyday
I became a worker on the unknown
But I understood one thing:
The footsteps on snow
Are blown by the wind.
A circle of illusions and delusions
That's life
Days passing by
Years passing by
So when they were saying
Life is a dream
They might have been right
Although no one is right or wrong
It depends on which side of the circle
You are standing
Or running.
I keep adding layers on my canvas
And life keeps adding years on me

Nothing disappears
But the latest layer of life covers the previous.
I am chasing purity
A white canvas is the best painting
Just like the best poem is silence
And the best symbol of the temperature of my heart today
Is snow covering the world.
While I think about all this
Allowing breaks for my inner voice to breath
I remember warmth raising from my chest yesterday
And I hear a cracking sound breaking the silence
A coup of black coffee exploding
Little kitchen fireworks
For the new year to come.
I might have been on the wrong side of the circle
when I started wondering about the temperature of my heart today.
So I wrote on a white canvas
And in a silent poem
Today's dreamy mood:
Train your eye to read signs
On the snow or in the kitchen.

BRAVE NEW WORLD

I moved to the brave new world, but winter keeps following me. As if some barriers were broken and my mood moved also to the brave new world: from inside towards outside. I spent most of the day reading and looking outside the window. I followed a dog jumping in snow and I tried to refrain my impulse to go ask him: would you like to be my dog? From behind the curtains, I saw the tanks coming back from the parade. Today is Romania's national day and I now live close to the tanks. In case of war, I am protected, the worst thing that can happen is to slip on the frozen stairs.

I went to a theater play a few days ago. The public opinion. And while defying wind and snow and freezing cold in the short walks I took around the neighborhood, I kept thinking about the words of an actor: don't blame the madmen cause they hold the sparkle of change. And I add: they see and do things that you don't have the courage to do. I kept walking till the last row of houses, where the dogs live, lost in the wilderness of bushes and poplar trees. My hand holding the cigarette was frozen, I could not feel my ears, but the only thing I thought of were the years lying in front of me. When faced with a critical situation, the same actor from the play said: I am not scared, what's the worst thing that can happen to me, I could die or my sparkle can gradually decrease.

And me, from the brave new world, I add: you can do as many magic tricks as you want, you can reinvent yourself everyday, dancing the never ending rope dance, but who is meant to stay unimpressed, will stay unimpressed.

I am dressing up for a party tonight. From the brave new world, I bring a sparkle.

THE CONCEPT FACTORIES

In my neighborhood, there used to be a factory named Freedom. So I imagined little boxes filled with the best quality export products: freedom leaving on ships to unknown lands. The factory kept running after communism fell, cause freedom has inertia, hasn't it? Nowadays, it has been re-branded, they sell seeds. Cause freedom grows in greenhouses, doesn't it? The Red Light District in Amsterdam was grown from one of these seeds: they received a little golden box with tulips carved on it and not knowing what they will grow, they planted it. The seeds of the wind of change were also created here and carry the guilt for all the storms in the world. In Romanian we say: *who plants wind will harvest storm.*

I passed by the factory named Independence and found it deserted. But it's true, you can be independent only in the desert. I kept walking, like an experienced walker that I am, trying to remember if a factory named Hope ever existed. And if it did, I hope I won't find it deserted. And then I remembered, the local football team is named the Will and every morning, the players train, doing little will dances, while running in circles inside the stadium.

And there is another important aspect about us, the locals, we have an association for Peace, on one of the little streets in the historical center. I spotted an old man opening the door and wondered how many associations in this world have only one member.

THE CAFÉ

You know that feeling
When you walk inside a bar, sit at the window
Take off your coat, light a cigarette
And order yourself a coffee
You started re-becoming yourself
The bubble is broken.
Or that feeling when you walk inside a bar at night
You are in a bar
In your home town
A stranger with a hat
A tourist at home
There is no one waiting for you at home
Life has changed
You light yourself a cigarette
You listen to the music played in the dim light of the bar
And you feel like dancing:
I can create bubbles
This is what re-becoming myself means.

THE LYRICAL TALE OF THE TREE

Since she arrived here on voluntary exile, in her little Siberia, she waited for the cold to paint a layer of ice over the world. In still mornings of the fall, she waited for the scratching sounds of steps on ice to raise from silence. Every morning, closing her eyes to catch a glimpse of the purple skies she visited while sleeping. Or those that she at least wished to visit. And then, the indifferent flow of a new day, a look outside towards the ocher leaves of a tree breathing during fall. A seasonal adornment, cause just like the humans, the trees lead a seasonal life. She wished to paint the tree, you so beautiful, you've grown ten meters since I last saw you, I have grown none, my tree. But at least, since I saw you the last time, I ceased to wish to become transparent, now I want to fix my image next to trees, to owls, to foxes. A tale of the wind scratched on canvas.

But as days go by, the image of her world stands still, sunk in silence. When cold finally arrived, she took her brushes outside to paint the ocher leaves of the tree. But the tree was now naked, no memory of the leaves, just wind blowing. The stormy breath of the world. When you turn away your look for a while and then come back, you realize something has subtly changed.

When she looked at herself in the mirror, she discovered her long hair has grown white.

As doubt gives birth to fear, as trees give birth to memories of knowledge, life gives birth to death. And who is afraid of living, will end up being afraid of death.

THE LYRICAL TALE OF THE STEPS

What she wishes for does not exist, but they say: be careful what you wish cause you might have it. So she ended up being the richest girl in the world, owning numerous imaginary wishes. Although, she now knows caring has nothing to do with possession.

Since winter arrived, she started heating up her socks on top of the oven cause wearing your bare naked thoughts in winter can be freezing. So she warms up her steps a bit, to leave a footprint of human warmth on the outside world. Since she arrived here, her steps carried her around the small town and everybody started knowing her. The waiters from her favourite café, the waiters from her other favourite café, the lady from the only shop selling tobacco and time. When you smoke a cigarette, you take a little step outside time, meeting all the frozen imaginary wishes. The lady welcomes her with a warm smile and tells her about beauty. But lady, what is beauty good for, since from the moment I step outside this magic shop, I go back to the frozen world.

The guy playing the guitar on the main street of the center befriended her, he waves hello when she passes by, because he now knows her. She stopped once to listen to him, a young guy, but strangely enough with white hair.

A ghostly vision of winter. She slowed the tempo of her steps to listen to him, cause she is in no hurry, she has all the time in the world to mediate upon her distorted relationship with time.

The lady from the wardrobe at the theater knows her, she said: I know you, you come here almost every evening, taking your front row seat and wearing this frozen look. Leave your frozen look here at the wardrobe and enter this magic world, wearing your warm steps only. It's warm inside the theater, she comes here for the laughter, the thoughts, the doubts, the questions and maybe for the human warmth that nourishes her hungry steps.

When walking back home, she thinks: everybody seems to know me here, everybody but me. So it is time to vanish, leaving the lyrical tale of the steps behind.

FAR AWAY

LIFE IS ON THE OTHER SIDE

I once stood on the seashore
Seagulls, cold and infinity
And I told myself:
Life is on the other shore.
Another time, I stood in a crowd
Bodies, warmth and pressure
And I told myself
Life is in another crowd.
Ages ago, I lived in a foreign land
Order, rain and distance
And I told myself
Life is in another land.
I once looked at myself in a mirror
Clarity, brightness, depth
And I told myself:
Life is in that reflection.
I walked here today
Cold, bodies, distance, depth
And I told myself
Life is on the other side.
There is no other side
I see it with clarity
It comes as an order

From the pressure of the cold,
But the infinity of seagulls need
Brightness to protect themselves from rain.

PAINTING GALAXIES AND THE UNKNOWN

I remember walking around the quiet town
Surrounded by a cloud a smoke
It could have been Magellan's cloud
Or just my personal numbness
My distance from one galaxy to another
It was raining heavily
But I couldn't feel a thing
Cause I vanished inside a cloud of smoke
I am an experienced walker
I walk away from reality everyday.
I remember I had the funniest idea
Sparkling from inside the cloud of smoke
What if
All these planets, galaxies
This universe.
Will cease to exist
When I cease to exist
When I learn something and there is no need for me to exist
Who could prove me when I cease to exist
That I am wrong.
As long as I exist, you can not prove me I am wrong.
Imagination is the sharpest logic

A knife in the hand of the distant
The experienced walker away from reality
A knife to cut down with
Questions from the sky.
It seems I started painting galaxies
As a remembrance of that fortunate cloud of smoke
And the unknown painted green
Cause I believe there is life inside the unknown.
And where do we go when we sleep
And whom I could ask all these questions.
I am not ashamed to say I don't know
I don't even know myself entirely
How could I know the universe
And me painting inside it.
My little universe
So distant from all the others
A three layered perspective
Going deep to the unconsciousness
Another unknown
And linking my shadow to the cloud of smoke
That could have been my personal numbness
Or a purple galaxy to cut down questions from.

THERE IS A WORLD IN WHICH

There is a world in which
I never left my home town
I walk to work everyday on the same streets I walked during high school
I work in a library
And live a multitude of imaginary lives inside my books
I always wanted to move inside a novel.
I go to the theatre every week
And gliding every summer
There is a world in which none of my friends left my home town.
There is a world in which I became a veterinary
I cure dogs and horses
And my cat never died.
There is a world in which no one
betrayed me
But there is a world in which I never met my friends
There is a world in which I became immortal at age 22
When time stopped suspended in darkness
I walk around with my eyes closed since then
Searching for the lightness of being.
There is a world in which I abandoned engineering in the third year

And I am artist since then
I write poetry for paintings
And I have courage.
There is a world in which I go on working at the university I did not have courage to abandon
Every day while walking to work
I pass by a shop named Time
Without buying anything
I go outside to smoke and look at the seagulls
Although Bucharest is far away from the sea
The university is also the set for a movie
They started with Closer to the Moon
And as years went by, I started involuntarily acting in some movies
Cause with my hat and detective costume
That does not fit anywhere else
I mingle well with the actors
I look at the seagulls and I tell myself
We are closer to the sun now, maybe.
There is a world in which I did not leave my country
And a world in which I did
There is a world in which from an attic
Where a seagull sometimes knocks at the windows
The neighbours still hear some strange foreign music and never ending arguments
And there is a world in which those arguments stopped
And music stopped
And silence walked in
And I am still there
Learning how to ride a bike.
There is a world in which I never
started painting at age 27.
There is a world in which I do not keep the future away

With one poem a day
In which I am not afraid of pain.
There is a world in which I vanish
I go see the big world outside
I start walking the real world
Country after country.
There is a world in which all these exist at a time
Mixed with the imaginary worlds
And there is a world in which I can distinguish between what is real and what is not.
And besides all these
There is the future
One of the many possibilities
Cause I am at a crossroad again
And you can enter the future through this painting
And see who is living inside all those houses
Imagining if there is a world in which…

DREAMS

THE MERMAID IN MY DREAM

I went to see a surreal movie
And while the main character
Kept falling asleep,
While the main character
Kept dreaming,
I fell asleep myself
In my velvet chair
Standing still in the darkness.
I remembered the most beautiful dog in the world
Standing still while having his hair combed,
I remembered a stray dog
Standing still in sunshine
Breathing next to his shadow,
I remembered a bird
Standing still on a windy day
At an unknown height in the sky.
I told myself once again
That the hardest thing
Is to live in present
In the momentary silence
Of your truth
Of your wind
Of your dreams.

I told all these
To the mermaid in my dream
The split woman
Half past, half future
To the half split sun
To the darkness
To the brightness.
And then I woke up
And went on watching the surreal movie
In which the main character
Kept falling asleep
And dreaming.

UNKNOWN LANGUAGES

I had a dream
I was walking around
And I met a beautiful lady
I couldn't see her face
Just like in my paintings.
Before the day when I opened a secret door
Towards imagination
A world where the only pain possible
Is the one you enjoy recreating
Cause it is glued to all the rest
A world where you become master and slave
Of your own repetitive emotions,
I had had a dream about me painting.
A new form of expression
In an old battle against silence.
I knew the lady was beautiful
A foreigner
Not speaking my mother tongue
Just like I am not speaking my mother tongue sometimes.
She was wearing a white mask
A stoned face
Time standing still for eternity
I could see her lips

Speaking a language I don't understand
Although I understood the meaning of her words.
She asked me about a place she wanted to take me to
But she did not know where it is in this land of mine
Only I could have known where it is.
She took my hand
A warm, comforting touch
A promise
Of companionship in life
For the hopeless romantics
To go on walking
Towards the unknown.
She could have been
Past or future
Or just time standing still on my face.
Fingers matching so well,
Just like in another dream
My voice was matching a voice that I don't know well
Yet.
The lady is me
I have met my stoned shadow in a dream
At last, making peace.
If you manage to balance
The sincerity towards yourself
With the sincerity to the world
If you manage to
Sleep naked
Dream naked
Wake up naked and walk around
Talking your naked thoughts
Even in unknown languages,
A lady witch visits your dream
And her hand makes a promise for the future.

THE DREAMS ABOUT TRAIN STATIONS

I have been having these strange dreams
Last night, I was in a big city with giant buildings
It could have been Den Haag
And I was in a house
My host was an old gipsy lady
Very kind, offering me everything for free
Her food, her house to live in
The only problem was that the house was close to the train station
And I know, train station areas are dangerous.
And then today, I dreamt
I was in a giant industrial area
With cranes, everything gray and silver
And I was followed by one of the characters in my paintings
The peacock
But this time, it had an owl face and a sharp beak
That could kill me
I took refugee inside a house
But the bird managed to enter
And I knew that the only escape for me
Will be when the bird enters a certain room.
The house was structured like a train

With only two wagons
One leading to the other
And above the entrance of that room
It is written:
Anima.
Your anima got attached to me
It's clinging to me
This is the power of the projection.
The bird should go where is belongs
And only then,
I will be able to take the train.
I am painting a departure
In my father's collection of disks
I found one
With a cover depicting a lady and a wagon
I will paint it
And add many colors
Depicting the vibration of my heart.

WALK ON THE BOTTOM OF THE OCEAN

I was on an open field
It looked like the bottom of the ocean
There were plenty of pebbles
As if a road was being constructed
Or at least something new
And I knew I should not be afraid:
The work was in progress.
It was all so white and free
And we crossed this immensity
And arrived in a village at dusk
It was smelling like summer evening
Just like on my balcony it smells like honey all the time
Some bees and flowers
And their work in progress
The day after I had this dream
I started painting cause I did not
feel afraid anymore
Whenever I am afraid of an emotion
I cannot paint
People think that if one has an emotional nature
There are only good emotions or sweet nostalgia
But you don't want to know
How frustration feels like

For the sensible.
But what do I know what people think
What do I know what is there at their bottom of the ocean
If they can cross it light heart-ed or not.
I painted in red and blue
The woman with her feet in the water
And the woman with her head in the clouds
The woman that carries the light in her fire costume
And the woman that is a house herself
And a bridge for both of them to walk on
When they will meet at the bottom of the ocean.

EGO

VANITY

I have a dog
I named him Ego
I walk him around the neighborhood every evening
We went to see the sunset
The third magnificent sunset in a row.
I took a portrait of him yesterday
Dressed in the blues and reds of sunset.
I feed my dog
Whose name is Ego
Everyday
But I must be very careful
About what he eats
He is very sensitive
If he eats something rotten
He goes wild.
I am not the only one feeding him
Although I pay so much attention
To his moods
I cannot control his diet entirely.
I try to teach him many things
Today I talked to my dog
Whose name is Ego
About vanity

Vanitas vanitatum omnia vanitas.
I told him we cannot posses anything
Not even our moods.
And if I think about it, Ego
You used to have a brother
He never died
But he kept hiding from us
He was the most vain of us all
So I will try to be sincere with you
I sometimes look at you
And I remember him
Dancing on a rope
He was a performer at the Vanity Fair.
So look, Ego
On today's canvas
I painted a radiography of you
Next to your brother
And I painted
Another case of duplication
On your right
Green man sitting
Thinking
And green man flying
What was the name of that Egyptian god with a bird's head?
I know it, of course
But I want you to remember it
And remember your brother
Who was the most vain of us all
Because hiding is vanity.

LEFTOVERS FOR A KING

Do you remember
I once wrote a poem
About a dog I had
Whose name was ego
Today I wanted to write a new poem:
Leftovers for a king.
I was walking around and in the courtyard of the Royal Palace
That is now a fine art museum
I saw a dog
I don't know how he ended up there
He has been locked inside at night
So I said
Hello Ego
He waved his tail at me
And we walked
Each of us on one side of the fence
Of that fine art museum
I like museums
They remind me color exists
I like getting lost inside them
Pass the gate and from the same side of the fence
Say

Hello Ego
Do you remember those books
Sense and sensibility
Pride and prejudice?
I am writing a book for you to eat
I will call it
Leftovers for a king
You will never accept this
You would rather die of hunger
Instead of eating
You prefer to write on a sheet of paper:
Hunger
And then chew that piece of paper
And still starve.
So listen, Ego
I don't know how we are getting out of this museum
We are trapped
It seems to me that every path we take
We end up in the same place
And you are hungry, Ego
I know this
And I might also know how we can escape
We write on a sheet of paper
Exit
And we exit
We abandon these leftovers for a king here
And when we get outside
We write on a sheet of paper
The art of living without my dog whose name is ego
And we chew it.

HUMAN INTERACTIONS

FRIENDSHIP

I remember how I befriended you
Because I saw something in your eyes
That we might be alike
But I couldn't tell at that time we were to share all these years
Cause at every age I had a dearest friend
To share my passions and my dreams
Or aches, if any
But you stayed the longest.
I remember all the people that we met
With whom we sometimes shared a table with
Or a life
And I see them gone now
But it's still you and me
And poetry
And a life lived to tell and to believe in something.
All the talks we had
and the light ways of passing from the difference between coke and pepsi
To the meaning of life
If it's expanding the consciousness or love.
From all the people I know
You are the one that matches best my romanticism

All the poetry we wrote
For lovers, ex-lovers or imaginary lovers.
From all the people I know
You are the only one
That made me a character in a novel
And I remember me fighting that beast that called himself a man
Because I care for you deeply and I wish no one hurts you
And they don't know you like I do.
I remember all the books I gave you for all your birthdays
Cause for me a book with something handwritten on it
Is a sign of affection.
I remember how we both escaped into visual
When words sunk into the ocean
And I remember calling you from far away
Just to let you know
That now I know, love exists.
Life is all about sharing
And if you have a friend to discover it with
Or to run away from emotional vampires with
You are not alone.
I remember the many drinks we had until the morning
Your batman costume on the beach in Den Haag
And the latest new year's eve we spent together
How I left and I came back
And everything we passed through a bit out of phase
But this friendship and its out of phase similar emotions is the only case I know
Of balance in similarity.
And now even if I will have to leave again
I promise I will come back.

THE STORY ABOUT TWO MELTING STONES

I must have read too many expressions up lately
I feel like melting
I must have wasted my energies in 1001 directions
Telling stories about two stones
I feel like standing still
And finish at least one of them
About the pattern people's expressions follow
From amazement to disgust
To infatuation
From grief to struggle
To resignation.
I would put a smile on top of the stones
But not glued to them
Somehow floating
Like when you fill your lungs with air
And you remember you are alive
To observe their expressions
And traduce them into stone.
I do not know more things about life then you do
In fact, I might know less
I am not even sure
That the expression of these melting stones
Will not change

As the time I spent waiting for a change will come to an end.
Whatever the art, it is merely a way of expression
And some might confuse it with the purpose itself
It is very simple
And this is how the story about two
melting stones ends
The purpose is just living
And this conclusion is engraved not on those stone faces
But on the smile shaped air floating on top
It is up to your imagination
To live well.

STABILITY

At times, I am so curious
Insatiable
I want to see what you see when you close your eyes
What moves
And what stands still
What kind of birds you hear
If the sounds gets decomposed
If the colors become fluid.
I sometimes close my eyes
And while everything spins and turns
I ask myself
Who dances behind your eyelids
And if there is anybody watching
And if they can describe it as I do
If they can pick up emotions
And while spinning and turning
Transform them into birds and colors
Then superimpose them
And send them back to you
Saying:
This is how dizzy you got when you danced
This is the only thing I know it's stable:
This is the layering of reality.

MANY NOTES TO SELF

I should learn how to fairly delimit myself
To say this is my eye and this is yours
My eye is a sensitive organ indeed
It absorbs light and darkness
And I feel that light and that darkness
Oh-so-strongly
My pupils dilating
My pupils contracting
Your fear
My fear
They should not mingle
Until I am sure
Which one is my eye
and
Which one is yours.
I am an emotional sponge
That gets heavy with darkness
And lighter with light
Of course,
Lighter.
I want to see better
To see where the border between justice and justice falls
Like dawn falling

Like dusk falling.
I should learn how to see clearly
And then I will write a clear poem about my eye
About its emotional capacities
About its symbolism
And another poem
About squeezing a sponge
Colors dripping out of it
A poem about how to squeeze a sponge
At dawn or at dusk.

MAYA AND WILL

THE JOURNEY OF WILL

When I left on this journey
I did not know what was pushing me forward
But I did leave to find my true nature
Whether emotional or intuitive.
My frail being was split
Between the sensual and the idealist
I was threatened from all sides
As if my skin was just a border
Between you and you.
I kept traveling
Looking outside the window
I could see the colors turning bright and violent
Light bulbs erupting under my skin
Light bulbs erupting outside my skin
I have seen myself so frail
Trying to stand still in the wagon that was carrying me
Pushing me forward.
I remember when I first stepped inside
I said my name is Will
And I would like to make a decision about my skin
My name is Will, but still I don't know who I am.
Days passed and from my window I could see many things

But all I was doing
Was to question myself about love
Trying to make peace between the sensual and the idealist
My name is Will and I could become a fierce full judge
While trying to protect the frailty of
my being.
I am Will, a poem inside a landscape
I see my reflection in the window of the wagon that carries me
The wind softly blowing the curtains
Everything becoming clear and transparent
The colors lost their violence
Everything so pale and frail
Like my skin
Everything so calm now
And I can finally make a decision
I am not coming back.

IF YOU EXIST, MAYA, THEN I EXIST AS WELL

I was five years old when I flew for the first time
I was coming back from the kindergarten with my mother
I was running
When I started getting detached
My feet moving faster
Me lifting
And I got scared
I had to come back, to stay grounded.
I still remember the place where I flew for the first time
I passed by today
And I smiled
I am not sure it is a real memory or a product of my fantasy
-between you and me it is the veil of Maya-
I kept lifting throughout my childhood
While standing in bed, I felt my body getting detached
And me getting scared again of never being able to come back.
If they would have put a brush in my hand
I would have been gone far away now
I had a rich inner world that remained a secret

I can still remember my childhood fantasies
And the superior way of adults talking to children
As if they understand nothing
And I knew so many things
Especially about flying.
-Dear Maya, sometimes I am not sure if I dream or not-
I kept flying in my dreams all my life
In my dreams, the sky was my playground
Some might say it is a sign of the need for protection
Of a thing that no managed to give me: comfort
Because the higher you fly, the more scared you get
But I secretly knew that only in the sky you can sometimes see the sun
Breaking a veil.
-when you go to sleep, do you take off your veil, Maya?-
I was seventeen when I first flew with a glider
A peaceful, birdlike sensation that I knew so well from my previous attempts to get detached
Between two flights, I used to pick up flowers on the field
And we had to be always careful at landing
Because of a shepherd we shared the runaway and the flowers with
And yes, this was reality
-Is it translucent your veil or does it make you see things foggy, Maya?-
And today, Maya, I became so aware of you
-Your breasts looking like mandalas-
Because I am not sure anymore
If I dreamt or not
My memories gained a foggy consistence
If I superimpose a painting and a photograph
If I add a lot of blur
I can see that veil of yours breaking at corners

And this means I became even more aware of it
-if you exist, Maya, then I exist as well-
I passed by the place where I first flew when I five
I saw myself as a child suspended in the favorite playground: the sky
And then I went to sit on a bench in the main square
I looked at people
And tried to connect to their reality
To what life means to them
And I couldn't
And I got scared again
Just like when I was a child lying in bed
And my body was getting detached.
This night, when I went to sleep
I found comfort in covering myself with your veil
Because between me and you
It's only your veil, Maya.

WILL SAILING AND EXPLAINING THE STRUCTURE OF LIFE

In life, there are two main approaches: one can go with the flow or can fight against it. In times of passivity, the awareness of the immense energy of the flow is dominant. The energy of the flow is however high at any times, but in times of action, the point of view changes. An inner energy is activated. The name of this process is enlightenment and it related to the fact that individuals passing through this process start glowing in a peculiar way. When this happens to imaginary persons, the glow is even more obvious. Other people prefer to use the word "will" instead of enlightenment. Words are very powerful, we are the ones giving them value. Imagine you can create an entire world with a brush. It is the same with words. Not every one paints, but everybody speaks. Use words with care, because there is life in everything we use. Our life. My name is Will and the girl that invented decided to call me so because I have this power: I sometimes glow at night. However one prefers to call it, enlightenment or will, it refers to a process that gives direction to an excess of mental energy we all have. If we use it unwisely, it turns against ourselves. If we send it outwards and use it for the creation of new worlds for example, what we previously called enlightenment or will, we could call now magic. If I manage to go against the flow and not drown, the girl that invented me will change my name to Magic Will. But for now, I am just sailing in this water and I sometimes glow at night.

WILL AT THE TRAFFIC LIGHTS

Will, do you like real people? Cause sometimes I don't. Maybe this is why I invented you. You could be a substitute, an excuse or a bridge, yes, a bridge. Do you like acrobatics, Will? Would you lye on your back, put your palms under your shoulders, ground your feet on real land and raise. Would you be my bridge, Will? Would you send a message for me to the real world? Would you let my thoughts walk over you? Like gentle caresses. Would you let them pass over you?

I walk around with you everyday, sometimes you show up at the traffic lights and wait there patiently. The red lights getting stronger, changing from just a red human shaped sparkle to a blinding red bulb. You wait and stop, so patient, as if all life is about waiting. How long does an imaginary life last?

At times, you accompany me at the theater. You don't look so unreal there. You sit in your velvet armchair, with the same patient air on your blurry face. You hold a cigarette in your left hand and you smoke with slow motions gestures. When you breath out, the whole stage gets filled with smoke. And that is the time when I think it is time for you to become real. How strong are you, Will, can you break this veil covering our eyes? Do you know Maya, Will? I won't ask you if you want to dance with her, I would ask you just where would you do it? Can you imagine this? Can an imaginary being imagine something? Could you be independent, Will? Can I be?

WILL AT PORT SAID

It's early morning and on the field that lays in front of me I see a worker dressed in white running. I sit in my balcony surrounded by plants and I light myself a cigarette with a cannon shaped lighter. I feel like leaving for Port Said. I don't remember which day of the week it is and I don't care about that too much. I started receiving guests in my imaginary world. To my right, on a wooden chair that reminds me of the roots of some trees. There is Will sitting. He looks very thoughtful. His transparent hands mirror my gestures. He light up a cigarette with the cannon shaped lighter and with an indifferent look, he asks me: did you finish that novel about the bohemians? When are we leaving for Port Said? Be patient, Will. Will power is not everything in life, although without it, you wouldn't have existed. We will leave for Port said soon, but only after we finish our cigarettes. The worker dressed in white stops for a moment to rest, he takes off the bag he was carrying on his back and he looks up. On the third floor balcony, there is Will smoking, surrounded by plants. He recognizes him and waves discretely to him. Then, he puts his bag on his back again and he goes on running.

WILL MEETS THE HIGH TIDES

When I reached the seashore and looked at the high tides
I couldn't tell what was purple and what was blue
If the sea was purple or blue
If the sunset was purple or blue
If I was purple or blue.
I couldn't tell the meaning of high tides, sunsets and journeys anymore
I kept quiet for a while
For fear I would lose my inner voice.
I looked for a while at the high horizon
At the foggy clouds of the future.
I looked for a while at myself.

WILL, THE BUSINESSMAN

The girl who invented me told me today:
Will, go and buy three canvases, a tube of white paint and some line-seed oil
You go and do all these for me
Cause I am just lying here in bed trying to imagine some strategies
Will, please do all the business for me
Cause I am already tired and I am not the most down to earth person I know
I would just stay at home and paint portraits of you for the next six months
I would paint you walking on the victory road
I would paint you ill and confused
Gazing at a sign saying that from here the road could take you anywhere.
Will, you are my favorite business man
So please go and buy me three canvases, a tube of white paint and some line seed oil
And let's paint some windows in the sky
And let's go on doing imaginary business
Cause without you, I am nothing,
Will.

MAYA AND WILL, THE ESSENTIAL QUESTIONS

I have many questions for Maya
To address to Will
About her veil
About the border between sincerity and hypocrisy
About the thin layer between conservation and abandon
I have many questions for Will
To address to Maya
About the necessity of a strong ego
To torture and to save oneself
About will power
And the irrational power
That can cover yourself
If you are not strong enough to torture yourself.
I have a question for both Will and Maya
Why do you live inside my head
And keep writing poetry to each other
When I should address questions only to myself:
What do I know about the things I don't know?
I tried to be humble
And while they kept chatting
I looked away from the mirror
I took my veil off

I said: Will, don't be stubborn, go to sleep
Look away from the mirror, Will
Cause there is your true power: outside.
While I tried to become humble
Will and Maya
Kept talking
Louder and louder
Will was playing god
And Maya as well
They took over the town
And panic was created
Cause when the essential questions are raised
No body can play indifferently
With the personal image reflected in the mirror.

MAYA TALKS TO WILL

Do you know that feeling when you come back to a place after one month and nothing seems familiar anymore? The giant plants took over the city, the weather is hot. You overlook the cityscape from a terrace at night and everything you can think of is that it is full moon again and you feel as if you descended from a dream. You say to yourself: eyes of a blue dog, remembering Garcia Marques. The last reality you knew is blowing in the wind. And you say to yourself: listen to the wind blow, remembering Haruki Murakami. Without magic we are nothing, Will. What do you prefer: a touch of unreality replacing the world as you knew it or the consciousness that you are dreaming? All I can say is that I like the eyes of the blue dog, I can read everything into them, I can read the wind blowing and the trace of your thoughts in the wind. Despite my emotional appearance, it is your mind that fascinates me. That is what I see in the eyes of the blue dog. Without words we are nothing, Will.

WILL QUESTIONING OUR ROOTS

Sometimes I sit in my room and I think about how many people feel alone, how many people would like to discuss painting, literature, Jung's psychology, Buddhism, Saskya, yoga, astrology, the meaning of life. We cannot be just leaves blown in the wind, Will. How could I meet those people? I think about all this and then you walk in, you start talking about our roots, where we come from and where we are going. I open the window, I see the trees in blossom and I tell you: pain is necessary, it opens the path to spirituality. And I want to tell you one more thing: when you happen to see a madman on the streets, just think that he might be an uncured idealist, or a monk that got too close to God or if madness got attached to a woman, think that she might have gone mad after suffocating the loved ones with her love. That woman wearing a veil might be Maya. Tell me, Will, what is the difference between a real friend and an imaginary friend? None, you say, this is how powerful the illusion is. I move around the room and as I get close to the window I think about your words. And I ask myself: should I trust my imaginary friend? Should I trust that piece of soul I put inside you when I painted you?

THE ART OF THE CONFUSED

THE MARCH OF THE ELEPHANT

I wander if anybody thought about the resemblance
between the wrinkled skin of an elephant and the surface
of a comet.
I wander if they have at the circus an elephant named
Churyumov
And a team of acrobats do scientific research
While fixing chords and harpoons
On the main valley of his back.
The elephant sings and dances on electromagnetic
rhythms
He orbits the stage with the grace of a well lit elephant
But even stars die and so do
elephants and comets.
I wander if people know how an elephant unemployed at
the circus dies
Elephant Gerasimenko goes alone in the desert
To follow the circuit of nature
To rebecome comet dust
Like all wrinkled skin creatures do.

LUCID DREAMING

Some days ago
During the full moon
I was sleeping
And I had a lucid dream
I knew I was dreaming
During the full moon
I woke up
And I had fever
And I told myself
Beauty disappears
When you move
From ideal to human.
I told myself true nostalgia
Is like wishing for the impossible
For the things you never had
And never will.
I had fever
And I started writing
More poems
Simultaneously
Like broken thoughts
About what being human means.
I finished none

And I still have fever
And I remember vaguely
About a lucid dream I had.

THE POEM ABOUT THE LION

In the past days
I've been like a lion in a cage
I feel like one important barrier is going to break
– the climax –
I tried to paint on the balcony
It was so hot outside
I kept wetting my forehead with cold water
Nothing is working
I cannot lead a thought to the end
– I want to know how much is my fault and how much the fault of others –
Only when I finished the first layer
I realized how much fury I have accumulated
And the thunderstorm started
I kept wetting my forehead with cold water
And I remembered I once wrote a poem
Break the weakness chain with beauty
So I told myself:
Dear lion
Stop biting your tail
Write a poem about rage:
A lion in a cage
Was affected by rage

He walked on the stage
And he turned the page.

SELF PORTRAIT

Portrait of a woman
Split between the sensualist and the idealist
Between the inner and the outside world
Between imagination and reality.
Portrait of a woman and her introverted feeling.
Portrait in harsh lines
Of a woman
Split between her desire to live and her desire to dream.
Portrait in red and green
The colors of all complementary passions
Of the visible half of a woman.
Self portrait.

A NEUROTIC MONA LISA

I am hungover and nostalgic
It is hard to keep your integrity when everybody wants a piece of you
I have been under siege up lately
They said: honey, open up your mouth
And let those beautiful words of yours come out
Let me come in and deposit my ideal inside you
Cause I don't know you
And this is why I want you.
They said: I see sadness in your eyes
And I said: you are afraid to look inside the mirror.
Knowing all these mirror games is what makes me solitary
I trust nobody but my hands
And their power to create
And their power to destroy.
Cause I know what makes me human
Is my capacity to hope or to disintegrate
I am both spiritual and promiscuous
I am both Doctor Heart and Patient Lust
A neurotic Mona Lisa
And I fight a hard battle against myself everyday
So do not deposit your hopes inside me

Just filter the medicine that comes out from my private war
And don't accuse me for the poison
Cause bees and wasps are the most natural thing
Don't accuse me for failing your ideal
Cause the further away you are from me
The less you know me.

WHAT IS IMPORTANT

I have such a strong personal filter
At times it is hard for me to understand
What is important for me to catch
If a ray of light is important to catch
An upside-down silhouette
Which I do not know where is belongs
If it is from another painting
As if it were from another life
Or it is a ray of light shining here
Where borders dissolve
Where I put my left hand
Trying to break a veil that I now understand
Whom it belongs to
It is mine
I am the veil itself
And I wonder what I try to cover
As I go on painting with my left hand
I found out with surprise I might be ambidextrous
I could both catch and cover
I am always on the edge
Where everything is transparent
At times it is hard for me to understand
What is important to catch

Where does the light come from
From inside or outside.
As I put my left hand inside the painting
I see it transforming from a ray of light
Into some harsh blurry lines
And I understand
Imagination and reality have different sizes
One is bigger then the other
But in order to go on painting
In order to go on catching light with my left hand
In order to go on covering light with my left hand
I should preserve the light of my consciousness.

THE DISQUIET OF LEAVING AN IMAGINARY WORLD

Yesterday afternoon I have been watching a video about dolphins giving birth
And I almost felt sorry they didn't go on functioning as only one being
During all this time, disquiet started growing around me.
Then I watched a video about lions meeting their human friends after a long time
And I wept a bit, how silly of me, they should have never parted
During all this time, disquiet was growing around me
I should go on functioning as only one being
I should never depart from myself.
I put this disquiet into lines and colors
The geometrical tears of a dolphin
In water
A dolphin with the brave heart of a lion
Still swimming
How silly of him
Swimming
As if standing still
Inside his own disquiet.

FEAR OF ELEVATORS

Whenever I have many things to say
But I can utter none
I take a brush and start mixing colors.
Today I had sunlight on my canvas
And I thought about many things
Short thoughts like flashes of light on a canvas
And we all know light is too fast to catch.
I thought about one morning when I sat on a bench facing a lake
About a walk in the forest with my parents when I was little
About a late evening among quiet people and a white cat
About why I am afraid of elevators
And how come there was a time when I completely forgot about this
If I want to express my fears, my memories
The things I understand and those I don't
I take a brush in my hand
And I start mixing colors
If I have sunlight on my canvas
It's even better
Because then, I can express my hope.
I sometimes feel disappointed

Cause from this closed world of mine
Understanding is missing
And that is my biggest longing
I understand myself more then ever
In these times when I must appear the maddest
But only my understanding regarding myself is not enough.
Average is an abstraction
It exists only in theory
But some people are just having bigger oscillations from what the theoretical average means.
We are out of phase with others most of the time.
And when we are out of phase, we are alone.
This painting shows my fear of elevators
And my lack of fear of putting my fears and dreams on the internet
Cause when I appear the maddest
I am actually the most aware of myself
And how little things I need to be happy
And how they are missing.
An elevator is a closed space
Just like my world is a closed space
An elevator brings you up and down
According to your choice or the one of others.
When I take a brush and start mixing colors
And have sunlight on my canvas
I become aware of my inner world as an elevator
And my fear of getting stuck inside myself
And my desire for understanding
As a door opening to the world.

BLUES AND LIGHT

I wondered
Where I come from and where I am going
If I should look inwards or outwards
If I remember well the past
If I can cope with the future
I asked myself why I feel split
Where does self doubt come from
Where is it going.
And then one day,
I put blues and light in the same image
I listened to my poems
I found them strange and distant
I thought about time
Last week sometimes far away
Months ago so close
And I wonder where this feeling of peace comes from
And I understood
In months of self doubt
I managed to unify my desires
And turn my gaze towards the future.
If I put blues and light in the same image
It means I don't feel split anymore
And the river,

That my words are,
That my paintings are,
Is getting bolder and brighter.
My fears are turning pale
Cause it takes a lot of courage to fight against oneself
Because inside you it's not only you
But all the people that you met
They live there
And one after the other
You shut up their voices
My river,
That is my words
And my paintings,
Is only getting bolder and brighter now
Cause freedom you conquer every day
Step by step
In battles against oneself.

FORGETTING

Forgetting is like a train that carries us forward
But we should know first what we forget
So that when we meet in a dream
When we open a door
And we sense a familiar scent
To know whom it belongs
Who got away with half of you
At some point of your life.
As we travel on this rail they call life
We gently pull back that part which used to belong to us
Saying:
I remember what I forgot
I remember you as I remember myself
But I am riding in this train they call forgetting
Because I want to live.
And life will open up in front of me
As the hand of a man looking for my hand in a train station
A man who opens up my heart as if I am 17 again
A time that I remember
As the time when forgetting was not necessary.

THE POETRY COSTUME

Take off poetry
And put it in the wardrobe
Like any other costume
And from the box
Choose another personality to wear
Hoping they will not notice
Remember that text of Julio Cortazar
About a man walking a normal life
And wandering if he is the only one seeing the monster here.
Take off poetry and hang it in the wardrobe
And hope they will not notice
You have been wearing fire.
Trying to sell that costume
Is like trying to sell your tattooed skin to a museum
To keep it on display
As a remembrance of the art of the confused.

DREAMLIKE CONSISTENCY

I went to sleep in this bed
I used to sleep here years before
I never wanted to leave
But I did.
I went to sleep
And I tried to move my gaze
Over these ten years that passed.
I tried to grasp my old dreams
What I wanted
And what I became
What is left to dream about.
I went to sleep and I walked these years again
As if you put sugar in a cold coffee.
I am unchanged only
In my dreamlike consistency.
I swing
Between fever and projection
Asking myself
If I tried too much
Or if I did not try enough.
I went to sleep in my old bed
I dreamt about many things
Like sunsets or time passing

I dreamt about people carved in stone
One of the most exquisite ways
To capture their dreamlike consistency.
And when I woke up
I was swinging on the edge of reality
I told myself
I must have dreamt about everything
And where I am swinging now
Is just the edge between fever and projection.
I went to sleep in this bed
Where I used to sleep years ago
And when I woke up
I told myself
I have a healthy dreamlike consistency
Which I advise you not to touch
Because it is contagious.

THE INCREDIBLE SADNESS OF THINGS THAT CANNOT BE CHANGED ANYMORE

FAIR PLAY

You build something
And it might crack
I could easily say
Stop building
But I won't do it
The cracks were there from the beginning
It's more obvious in black and white
You see the ribcage well
It is not called a cage for nothing
And the head, it is missing from the photo
It is not missing for nothing.
I could say many things
But I will say nothing
In black
In white
I am fighting against myself
Because I understood I have a power
Both constructive and destructive
And I need to handle it well
With care
And with that head
Missing from the photograph.

DREAMS IN THE BACKGROUND

From my balcony
I follow with the eyes some birds walking
Why would birds walk if they can fly?
It's windy and I am listening to Nirvana
Yells before the silence.
I do not remember how normal people behave
I am talking to ghosts all the time
In my head
At night, in a bar
I keep writing imaginary letters
Addressed to a dream
I do not remember how normal people behave
What they talk about
I don't know why birds walk instead
of flying
And why listening to nirvana is about hearing yells.
Everything seems a dream to me
A case of repetition
Saying something all over again
Yelling
Walking
Birds and nirvana
I wonder if there is silence

Where normal people live
Or if they just keep their dreams in the background.

THE DREAMERS

Call them dreamers
Or dancers on a rope
At unknown heights in the sky
Or in the underworld
When the skies are covered by dark stormy clouds.
Call them dreamers when they will slip on ice
Cause they touch reality quite rarely
Call them dreamers when they will look you in the eye
And tell you something
Although they are never really quite there
You never know where they are
Where they got lost
Or where they escaped
Cause they always look for secret doors
To take a quiet exit
Or a glorious departure.
I wonder how many dreamers are out there in the world
And how different their dreams are
And if they ever meet
To analyze the dreams of each other.
And how many dreamers killed each other
For their brightest skies.
Find comfort in your dreams

And when one day you will eventually
Bring them into reality
You can start slipping on them
Cause you are a creator of ice
And clouds and storm
And go on dancing on your rope
At an unknown height inside yourself
You are a cloud machine
A dreamers creator.

WAR AND PEACE

Since the day I met you,
that river started opening again in my chest.
A river of tenderness and disquiet and attachment to the impossible
A river made of words and their reflections
A river made of colors
As if colors were something consistent
As if another body poured sadness inside myself.
I thought about the way emotions circulate between people
If there is an universal balance
The sum of all the sadness in the world equals the sum of all peace
Since that day, I am thinking about war all the time
And tenderness
As my chest that carries a river of words and their reflections
A river made of colors
As if colors were something consistent
My chest starts trembling
Because of a feeling I was always looking for
When reading novels Such as War and Peace.
My chest trembles at the sight of your hands shake

Because I do not know anything about war
But I am as well scared of sounds
I am afraid of music
Because it holds the key to that river I told about.
I always thought I carry a burden on my shoulders
Some kind of universal sadness
But I tell you the stand straight
As we measure the height of each other
Bare-feet
As if measuring the height of our expectations
Souls naked.
The day we met it was still summer
I have been smoking all day
And walking slowly towards you
You waved at me and it was as if I met an old friend
I knew the sadness in your eyes
Because it was mine also
I took pleasure in just looking at your handsome face
The pleasure of watching you talking
Or just being.
And then, a few days later
As you taught me abandon
Pleasure and comfort at the same time
I knew what word was coming first out of that river
Let's make this tender war every night
Let's just keep calling it so
Although it's the most peaceful thing
Let's just keep calling it so
For the sake of universal balance.

WE

I don't know how it happened
My arms opened and welcomed you
I kissed you on the cheeks
A very erotic touch, indeed
And then we looked at each other
It was a very intense gaze
I could sense your legs moving
But our eyes kept touching
A very erotic touch, indeed.
This night we said we for the first time
And we kept looking at each other
Having wine and laughing
We kept saying we:
We like a good talk and sunny places
We like the touch of silk and looking outside the window in winter
We might like each other.
And my arms opened and welcomed us for the first time.

THE HEART IS THE CENTER OF THE UNIVERSE

You try to understand
You turn to psychology
To your childhood
Parents and ancestors.
You look at the stars
Galaxies and neuroscience
To search for connections
Thinking about the vibration of your steps on earth
You think about this new theory
You were almost about to develop
And about that little girl painting next to her cat you once saw in a photograph
You think about Anna Karenina
And all the art in the world as a product of misunderstanding
The more you try to express that thing,
The more you understand how it is slipping between your fingers
Just like that day when with your eye closed
You almost caught the meaning of the illusion
Before it vanished again
In the deep space of your own neuron-connections

In the deep space of repetition
A rehearsal room
Where all your ancestors were trying to recreate life
With or without understanding the meaning of that thing
That almost made you develop a theory about vibration
In connection to probability
And a very unscientific matter
Named luck.
The way your heart vibrates is a matter of mystery
So you could take up to writing detective stories
Instead of turning to geophysics
To understand the way your steps vibrate on earth
You understand your body as a host for a holly thing named rhythm
And you try to understand
Maybe it's a matter of hormones
Time ticking inside you
Faster and faster
Until the stampede of feelings just stop
Before they start galloping again
To go find a new religion based on vibration
Or just ancestors
And the repetition of that thing
You are not going to pronounce.
So after trying to understand it
From very different viewpoints
From outside and inside
After using many kinds of tools
To build it or to destroy it
I understand I do not understand anything
It remains a mystery.
And the cycle repeats
Because this is what vibration is about.

To say that the heart is the center of the universe based on vibration
Is not just a poetic statement
But some scientific intuition that was not demonstrates it
Which applies at least for me
Since this is my universe.

TO THE MAN I LOVED

I carry a feeling in my chest
A bird or a crystal
I do not know what to do with it
I tried to kill it many times
To paint it
To write it
To just let it it be.
This feeling is uplifting
So pure
So strong
Some might call it madness
But I do not know how to call it
Since I cannot even paint it
Or write about it
While carrying this feeling in my chest
I wish I could invent a language
To send it as a present to you.
This feeling
So pure
Has nothing to do with possession
Or jealousy
Or having you around
It has nothing to do with time

I find it tickling in my chest
At the same intensity
Every now and then
Sometimes for entire days
And I do not know if I should kill it
Because it is indeed uplifting.
The matters of the mind and those of the heart
Are two very distinct things
And I feel irrational
A very irrational woman
That wished to be your companion
And sometimes maybe to touch
Your hand and your chest.
I know you feed yourself with these words
And I also know that you never wanted me entirely
And knowing all these
I still carry that feeling in my chest.
I am afraid one day I will forget
Why I carry it with me
I will forget the words and the looks
And my memory will become fog
Leaving behind a detached emotion.
I started writing because I am afraid
One day I will forget who I am
Just like I forgot all the books that I read
A mad woman carrying a very pure emotion in her chest
And life as a novel hiding forgotten words
But not forgotten feelings.
Mad or irrational
Or just a woman
That had the chance to meet you once
And you set her free
To write and to paint for the world

When she only wished to paint and to write
Just for you.
Maybe the world will thank you one day
And me being part of the world
I should thank you too
Cause now I have more words and more colors
To express this world
That is mine just like I am part of it
But never enough to express the feeling I carry in my chest.
I tried to kill it many times
By practicing indifference
By searching for you in other people
But then I stopped trying to kill it
Cause I did not really manage anyway
So now I just live with the feeling I carry inside my chest
Instead of living next to you
Because this is how life goes
And I am no windmill fighter
I am no night train traveler
I am just an inventor of unknown languages.

FIREFLIES

This night I saw that somebody was throwing fireflies
over the window
They say that if it is pitch dark
you can see
The light of a candle from far away
A sparkle of all kinds
Of a thought
or of a desire.
It is not pitch dark
But raining
And I try not to let water pour down from my soul
I do not want to disintegrate
I do not want to throw away fireflies over the window
But I do.

THE DAY YOU LEFT

The day you left, I found myself on a cliff
I was tired and scared
The wind was blowing my coat
I was standing on a cliff
And I couldn't recognize the sea
It was winter in Ireland.
The day you left
I couldn't recognize you anymore.
I put my hat on and turned my back to the past
I pulled a shadow costume over my shoulders
So that you couldn't recognize me anymore.
The day you left
I saw a smile freezing on your face
It was very cold in Ireland
That winter.

THE DESIRE TO BE FREE

YOUNG WOMAN

Old man with your mouth shadowed
By a flying creature
A shadow itself
I see grief in only one of your eyes
The other eye duplicated
Detached
Looking outside.
It looks muddy this eye of yours, old man.
I put you in a portrait with a parrot
Like Frieda Khalo and her oh-so-many parrots
But I kept the parrot invisible
Because I have this magic power
If I close one eye, I can cancel half of the world.
I could send away flying the shadow covering your mouth, old man.
I wish a youngster came and
analyzed my paintings
Maybe Jung himself
To tell me how the primitives
Used to eat their totemic animals
Cause I see something strange next to you, old man
It seems to be a fox.
How strange.

Maybe the old man is just a young woman
That used to call herself wise
Just like an old man
Until they came and took away from her
Some roots
The wisdom tooth
Just like they would take away a baby painting
If only they could.
There is no need for a youngster
To come and analyze this baby painting of mine.
While uncovering the shadowed mouth,
I can analyze it myself
With this muddy eye of mine
Detached
Looking from outside
A young woman should stay a young woman
Leave the wisdom for the old.

THE DAY WHEN I DECIDED TO BECOME AN ACROBAT

The day when I decided to become an acrobat
Was the same day when I thought about quitting metaphors
Like a drug addict wrapped up inside his own emotions deciding to break free.
It will take me about seven years
To become an acrobat
And it might take a life time to quit metaphors
But only then my inner voice will become crystal clear.
Today I realised what a power I have
To put emotions into words
And how sharp it can become if I quit metaphors
If I manage to be equally sincere to the world and to myself
If I manage to become an acrobat in seven years.
The day when I decided to quit metaphors
I had the strangest dream
It was about the sea as usual
But this time there was a river flowing where usually the waves break
There were small arrows showing the direction of the river flow

It was just like a road you are on
That separates two fields
It was a metaphorical dream
About maybe what is the greatest metaphor
The day when I decided to become an acrobat I had a dream about life
And one day I will be able to explain it simply
when I will find the perfect balance between being sincere to myself and the world
One day I will be able to explain
How long it took me to become an acrobat.

BALANCE

I don't know if I am attracted to the strong or the sensitive
But one thing is certain
I am attracted to the impossible.
I am attracted to the possibility of keeping a perfect balance
Between strength and sensitivity
While keeping your weight on my shoulders.

HOME IS INSIDE A PAINTING

I want to be a creator
But what is a creator supposed to eat
I kept asking myself this.
A creator eats light.
So I studied the subtle changes of light
In a rainy day
Greys and pinks and something transitory
That is light.
But what I like to study the most
Is my heart
And I feel light heart-ed today
Although a bit restless
Like all the light eaters.
There is no other place like home
And home for me is inside a painting
Come visit the brightest chambers
Welcome to my mind.
There is where light is recreated
There and in the air around
Layers after layers of bright air
A mood laboratory
A colorful scenery
This is my mind.

Disregard the blur
Cause among the many chambers
There is one inhabited by clarity
A door leading to the straightest path
Towards the unknown.

A SUITABLE ISLAND SCENERY

Dear Jung,
Dear God,
Dear Haruki Murakami,
Now that I reached this border
Can I please burn all my paintings and start over new?
Cause truth be told
I love life better than painting
But life has betrayed me too many times.
If you want to kill all the artists in the world
Just take away suffering from them
It's very simple, I tell you.
In a world with happiness only
No one will find the need to express it.
Oh, my dear unconsciousness
How funny you are
Now you send me outside to live
Aren't you?
I cannot help laughing,
Life is a joke
Don't take yourself too seriously
It's bad for your health.
This is a painting about body, mind and spirit
Eyes, breasts and colors.

The observer
The woman
And the uncertainty.
I went to a party last night
As an observer
Don't you dare look me in the eye
I sat there watching people getting drunk
I watched myself lost between people, countries and emotions
Like any observer
That never really belonged to any place
My place is on an island
Whenever I needed one
I invented it.
I ended up with a drunkard
Sitting next to me
He told me drunkard stories
And paid me a surreal compliment:
You have two rows of upper teeth, dear.
I was watching life at a party
And I couldn't help laughing
How repetitive is everything
Just like colors forming a pattern,
How transitory.
And me with my stupid emotions
I ended up as an observer
Instead of laughing at life from the inside.
I found myself on the dance floor
Watching some images they were projecting on a screen
About huskies, trains in snow and Aurora Borealis
Colors forming a pattern.
It was a scenery suitable for an island I could invent.
But now my unconsciousness is making fun of me

Go out and live.
So I sit here
In front of my painting
Which I could say
That I somehow invited
I sit here
Laughing with my unconsciousness
At life.

THE MYTHS

TRY TO GRASP DISTANCE, I SAID

I had a painting with a mermaid in my studio
My studio is my balcony
From here I study myself and the passers-by
I tried to be sincere
While coloring my dyslexic emotions
So I asked myself
Who am I fooling
And then I covered the painting of the mermaid
In skin color
Nude beige.
I was smoking in my studio
Until the colors turned foggy
And I couldn't see the passers-by
My eyes were turning numb
So I told myself
Who am I fooling
No one can understand my mythological expectations
I thought about all these
While painting an underwater town
As if I was painting my surroundings
I am an island and everything around me is slippery
Try to grasp distance, I said
And try to give it a name:

Mermaid covered in skin color in the underwater town of dyslexic emotions
Obsessional neurosis
Love.

BUILDING UP A MYTH IN YOUR OWN ROOM

This bed is nothing but a nest
Where you can grow yourself
Colorful eggs of imagination.
You can grow yourself
By adding a layer of colors,
A layer of symbols
And so on
Cause the perception is infinite,
Though you need only one eye
To really see
Where exactly you are taking a rest.
Art is all about synthesis
Building up your own myth
On the roots of understanding.
Before moving on
To a new nest
To a new life
To a new you
You magnify those roots
Through a new age art
Called analysis
Or nudity.

You are building up a myth in your own room
By using all kinds of tools
Such as hands
Or heart
Or a dive into sleep
Cause dreams are nothing else
But companions of your expectations.
I said you
But you is me
Dreaming.
Remember, I have only one eye
Of infinite perception.

GOLDEN SHADOWS SWIMMING IN A RIVER

I have been waiting for a sign,
For a sound to break the silence,
I have been waiting for Godot to arrive
Although I never knew his face
I have been in love with the idea of love
All my life
The idea of love is greater then the love of human beings
It just gets materialized in a person
Like projecting some images on a screen
But when I close my eyes for a short second and then I open them again
I see there is no one around
And I am surprised again about this power that I have
That is called imagination.
There is a god inside me
Which is neither Sisif, nor Prometeus
But Platon
A master of ideas
And their projections.
I have been waiting for the idea of waiting to come
To shadow my life in the most exquisite way
A shadow that shadows a shadow
The perfect encounter of ghosts

And like all the ghostly matters
Incapable of shaping into reality.
I was granted a power and I had a god living inside of me
And I almost touched gold
Like King Midas
Until wind
That is life
Blew it away and transformed it into dust
We are mortals, so close to beatitude but never really touching it
We are gold separated from gold through wind
That is life.
I have been waiting for something to happen
To prove me that a shadow can indeed shadow another shadow
Until I understand you are not supposed to touch true gold
But to look at its glow
Just like looking at a river from on top of a hill
You see where it comes from and where it goes
You see the golden glows on its surface in a starry night
But you can see all these only from above
And when you go swimming inside that river
You will find yourself a strange animal
Completely golden but unaware of its shadow.
I have been waiting for another golden animal to come shadow the river with me
Until I got tired of waiting
Enough, I said
Damn you, Samuel Beckett, I am bigger than you
I can turn the direction of the flow of this river
Cause I believe the opposite of the absurd is the art of understanding.

GENUINE ART

You might call it outsider art
But I call it genuine
This is the thinnest mask a human can wear.
In my chest, where there was a golden cage
There is now a river
I do not know where it comes from
I just sit hear and record its flow.
I walked around yesterday and I saw a statue
Three drowned men
Stretching their arms to grab something
I imagined a river and a cage and a chest
And the fourth man
That is actually a woman
Recording the moment when the
cage opens and releasing the river
and the three almost drowned men,
Just like releasing some animals
Let's say
A lion
A donkey
And an eagle.
So I say to myself
Jung might have been proud

I transformed an ocean into a river
And I saved from death three almost drowned men
And I am woman
Wearing only a very thin mask
Like one of the glazes you apply on a painting
That glows beautifully at night
Especially in those nights when you release some prisoners from inside your chest.
The look of despair in their eyes
That is what genuine art is about
I am untrained
I don't do this for money
Or fame
I do this for the sake of understanding
For the hope of understanding
Cause those men almost drowned for feeling hopelessly misunderstood.

THE ANDROGEN

Yesterday night a group a dandies sat at our table
Noisy, beardy and shallow
All dressed up in excessive testosterone
In May all the hormones go wild
It's the spring feelings, my friend told me
And I couldn't help thinking about what keeps the world go on
It's an encounter between individuals
But it's more then instincts I believe
I always liked sensitive men.
A terrace at night is a colorful scenery
I see people's eyes lighting up
And then becoming hollow
I sometimes close my eyes and I think
You never know what for someone falls in love with you
If it's your voice or your hands
If it's your hope or one of the things you consider redundant.
Reality is made up of layers
I think about the dandies disturbing our intimacy
And I remember a man
His eyes lighting up from the darkness of the bar
Showing up at our table

And putting a golden sculpture in front of us
A clay androgen
And obsessively asking
If we recognize our feminine shape in it
I thought about the androgen's opacity
And about how a layer of reality
Becomes fully opaque when you fall out of love
And you never know what for someone falls out of love with you
And when it happens
If it is when the spring feelings start lighting up people's eyes
Or when you start to feed your sensitivity from a new layer.
Reality is translucent
We keep adding layers
To keep the world go on
To go on chasing a dream
Of a peaceful world
In which you can close your eyes
Not to hide their hollowness
But to highlight their sensitivity.
Yesterday afternoon I was sitting on the floor
Inside a new layer of reality
Windows wide open
To the world
There was a peaceful wind blowing the curtains
And I couldn't tell if it was coming from outside or inside
If I started falling in or falling out
If the androgen shape I must have dreamt of a while ago
Was golden or redundant.
I kept having wine with my eyes closed
Until I opened them again

And I found my feminine shape reflected over the neighborhood
Everything painted blue and pink
Like in a dream I had before I started painting
I took a piece of paper and I wrote:
Today's dream
And I added a date sometime in the future
As if time mattered.

THE DIRECTION

There are nights when I just want to put my head to rest
To lie down and close my eyes and give in.
Do you know how it feels when something is tearing you apart?
Passion on one side and stability on the other
They say there is a limit to human suffering
And after that it's only ecstasy left
The mystics know this
And they might also know that if you cannot change reality
You could change the way you see it.
I walked this road alone
Between two wise tooth extractions
I walked inside myself to make peace
While dreaming about war at night
The moment I close my eyes, I stop belonging to me
I do not know whom I go visit while asleep
If my dreamy being makes a promise to someone
That I have strength and no matter what road you take you will arrive eventually in the same place
I wish this self of mine that goes visiting people
Could encourage myself also
In those nights when I feel only like putting my head to

rest
Wrap inside myself, hug my knees
And stop rebelling against life.
On this road I walked between two symbolic acts,
The wise tooth extractions,
I gained a better sense of reality
And a better sense of imagination
While these two forces rise
They go to war against each other
Instead of making peace.
At night I dream about war
And during the day I paint the town as I please
I noticed the colors are getting bolder and brighter
I analyze all these
Why it is so
Trying to grasp reality
But I might be doing some mistake here
The only reality I know is mine.
I wish I put my head to rest and ask someone wise which way to go
To show me the direction
And I played a bit with my paintings and photographs today
I improved reality a bit
I modified the way I see it
And I ended up with two ladies perpendicular to each other
Or how they would call it in maths
Normal to each other
Their hands pointing to the same direction
So the mystics might be right after all
No matter what road you take
You will end up in the same place.

I go to sleep now
Maybe I will find out that meanwhile the war has ended.

HEADACHE OR HEARTACHE, GOD AND MAN ALIKE

There is an old legend saying
That at the beginning, God had a terrible headache
And felt alone
This is why he decided to create the world.
I thought all day about loneliness and various ways to cure it
Supposing loneliness as a malfunction
And excluding the possibility of creation of a world.
Does acceptance cure it?
Or one shuts up a call that is deep inside the nature
Of man and god alike.
No man is an island
But wishing too much and fighting battles against life itself
Will send you eventually to live on an island.
I never wanted to accept anything
Because for people like me reality is the devil
My imagination is my savior and my curse at the same time
I can imagine many things, especially feelings
This is how I end up with pains in the chest.
I felt alone and I had a heartache

So I decided it is time to create a world for myself
I decided to start painting
Everyday my world was expanding
Like a colored spider web
And when I had the setting done
I started telling stories about them
About mysteries of all kinds
I became a sort of a detective specialized in imaginary matters of the heart
And I find myself today
Sitting in the middle of my colorful web
Like a king spider, fat and translucent at the same time
A spider with a heartache
Addressing a question to god:
Do you still have that headache?
And what medicine did you take to cure that malfunction of yours
They call loneliness?
Was the world itself a medicine strong enough?
Is this what acceptance is about?
Should I go on creating worlds for myself or should I accept this world of yours?
Because I must tell you
This is indeed a very complicated matter
I might see it a bit distorted
A spider wearing some very special lenses
But I am not blind.
Loneliness passes through the heart
And I see it clearly
Because I have a very good imagination
Especially for feelings.
But I am not sure that my feelings are based on something real

Or they grew by themselves in my colourful web
I can go so far as to claim that the whole world is an illusion
But I know that would be the ultimate collapse of the world of an introvert
The end in which God's headache is cured
And spider web creators like me, get to escape the ultimate pain
The pain in the chest.

PAIN AND HEALING

THE PORTRAIT OF HUMAN GRIEF

I don't get along well with time
We had an argument once
And I ended up painting
And since I started painting
I started growing younger.
What's the use of doing a precise portrait
When you can push the button of a camera
And in a few seconds of something you don't get along well with
You can have the sharpest lines
The precision of the most difficult time to live in
The present.
So slippery.
This is not a self portrait
But a portrait of the air around me sometimes
Which is not only mine
Just like I am not the only one that once had an argument with time.
This is the portrait of a human feeling
Cause I started painting a series of human feelings
Painting time passing by
Or standing still.
This is the portrait of human grief

And I stay here
Looking at it
I see Dorian Grey
Another warrior against time.
I see myself
Telling this portrait
That is not even mine
You, grow sad instead of me.
I am a hedonist.

THE HEALER

Wake up every day and just like a sleep walker
Walk through your life
For five days in a week
Love Fridays and hate Mondays cause all your life is in between
Wait for retirement to have fun
When your body will finally match the age of your mind
But don't say this to anyone
It's a secret
Especially for yourself.
This is how life goes
But who am I to question this
When I could just show you pictures from holidays
When I did live
But not as good as in my imagination.
The best trips I had
Were in my room
Wishing.
I wish I go to Peru one day
So I bought myself an album of photographs
Although I don't really need to see
I always wondered how other people imagine things
If they see something or just hear their thoughts

If I were to take another trip
I would go for a visit in someone else's head.
I found a picture of a magic healer in my book about Peru
Blowing smoke over his tools
Smoke is life
Breath is life
Wind is life.
I wanted to paint him
But I had only a small canvas
So I concentrated on his face.
If you take something outside the bigger picture
You might end up with a distorted reality.
My healer turned up to look like a drunkard
Just like the 9 to 5 people could look like workers.
We are born with the future
And die with the past
And in between there should be faith
In something
Whatever that might be.
A drunkard could be a magic healer
Blowing away smoke
Or fire
Or just life
Cause life is smoke and fire
And the drunkard and the healer could have the same face
If you never wanted to die
You will never understand joy.

POETRY AS MEDICINE, ART AS MEDICINE

Poetry as medicine, art as medicine
Capable of curing the gap between body and spirit
Capable of creating bridges between reality and imagination
When you start raising questions
The healing has already started
Slowly building in the background
Without even noticing
The transparent bridge of understanding.
And if one day you need it
You can take the medicine
And slowly repeat it as a mantra
As if playing a recording of your own hypnotic voice.
Wisdom is not the definitive answer
It is a momentary state
But which has the transparency and fluidity of
The bridge of understanding.
If one day you find yourself walking on that bridge
You might find out with surprise
That questions grow answers
And you can start creating yourself
Some new age medicine
Poetry and art capable of growing wisdom

Because now you know
That pain is possible
And necessary.

PAINTING FOR PAIN HEALING

This is the pain in my right knee
But of course you cannot see it
It's my knee
And my pain
This is what abstraction is about.
But maybe you can imagine how it feels
How it comes and goes away
And how many shades of knee pains are out there in the world.
The delicacy of a knee pain
The sharpness of a knee pain
The hatred against a knee pain
The kindness for a knee pain
So many
That you might end up thinking your knee pain is human.
If I start walking how I should
Sleeping how I should
Forget how I got the pain in the knee
It will go away.
If I walk away from reality less often
Stop daydreaming
And get a nice brainwash
It will go away.

But I'd rather put some rainbow cream on it
A little dose of a magic drug I invented myself:
Painting for pain spotting
Painting for pain abstraction
Painting for pain healing.

THE POSSIBILITY, THE NECESSITY

There was an illusion growing inside my knee
Following me with the eyes wherever I went
It was a painful illusion
An insatiable illusions
I tried to feed it,
Feed your knee
So you can go on dreaming
About hunger.
I kept asking my knee
About what is real and what is not
But my knee
Kept smiling
A Cheshire knee.
I tried to step on the pain
That was growing inside my knee
Like you could step on the bug
That one day you became.
But I found myself walking on water
So instead of asking what is real or not
I started questioning my knee about
What is shallow
And what is deep.
How deep is the sea we all carry inside of us

How deep is your love for pain
Cause it is part of you.
And as I bow down in front the necessity of pain
Me, my shadow and the butterfly we live in now
I ask you one last question:
If you had a wisdom tooth
That was also painful
Besides being wise
And one day it had been extracted
Leaving your roots blown by the wind
One of those under water winds
That could drag you down
Or help you float,
Would you ask yourself this
Or am I the only one mad here
Next to my shadow, in the butterfly we live in now,
Would you ask yourself this:
What if
After removal,
my wisdom tooth will grow again
Would I accept this
Would I accept the possibility of pain?
Would I?

REPETITIVE EMOTIONS

X-RAY OF MY SOUL TODAY

If I were to do an x ray of my soul today
I would say
It looks precisely like this collage
I thought about many things at the same time
About an artist dilemma
What was there first the sensitivity or the wounds
I thought about repetitive things, disappointment and over reactions
I asked myself whether I enjoyed myself today
And where is everybody rushing
As if time is something to kill
And not to enjoy.
I thought about me smoking all the time and thinking
There are still things I refuse to think about
I though about the fact that an x ray of someone's soul
Can show what madness that person is prone to
And how we are all prone to madness of all kinds
And that the biggest madness is to refuse to think about this fact.
I thought about how expressing oneself in the most coherent manner
Is the best way to avoid misunderstanding
Disappointment and future over reactions

I thought about how complex the dynamic of human interactions is
How fluid is the human psyche
And how artists seem to be sculpting air in the end
Because they were either born sensitive and overreacted to wounds since then
Or the wounds are those creating sensitivity
I thought about how difficult it is to sit down and write a poem when one is happy
How one needs a downfall to be able to rise
Cause otherwise all would be in equilibrium
No colors
No air to sculpt
No x rays of the soul.
I started doing a series of collages about repetition.
They might all look similar,
But if you look attentively, they are different.
Just like a life situation might look similar at a superficial glance,
But in depth,
It's completely different.
The series is not only about repetitive patterns, emotions and situations,
but also about the importance of details.

THE CAUSE OF SADNESS

The day when I reached the cause of my sadness was not an ordinary day.. I was digging for it for a long time, looking for patterns in my emotional behavior, looking for signs of self-sabotage as if some parts of me went to war against each other. For me the creative process is always a process of understanding, I start from the abstract, go through symbolic and writing comes only as the last stage.

The cause of my sadness came like a silent revelation, while I was smoking on the balcony like every other day. Imagine there is a current inside your body that does not circulate well, imagine an army of little men going up and down your veins and imagine their ruler in times of revolution.

Imagine I wanted to start healing all of them so I started with the headquarters. The first signs of distress were in my mind. And then I went downwards and checked how my heart was doing. My heart was well, this is why it became inhabited by a man named Doctor Heart.

The hidden cause of sadness was in the essence of my femininity and I was self-sabotaging myself for years with my attraction to the impossible. This hidden cause of sadness is strongly related to the desire to create because the creative process is also a healing process, although at the beginning I didn't know what exactly I was healing. Only when I understood this, I was truly ready to let my inner voice speak to the world because I know there are many people out there who have some problems with inner floods.

For a second there, I felt like I reached a harbor where everything is quiet and peaceful. I take a deep breath of fresh air and prepare to move further because all these revelations that we have are like train stops, we stop for a while and then the train that carries us forward goes on moving.

At night, I had a dream. The children I dreamt about some days ago appeared again. But this time they were condensed only into one. A child with only one amber greyish eye in the middle of the face. An eye looking beautiful and sad and wise at the same time. A child with many hands as if all the others condensed into him. A symbol for the unity of perception and the desire to deliver meaning and comfort to the world.

ART

THE THIEF

Some years ago a thief visited my house
I was sleeping and dreamt about
Somebody being inside the house
I tried to wake up
But I kept waking up
In a new dream.
Eventually, I said in a loud voice
There is somebody inside the house
I see a blue light.
Shut up,
I told you so many times
You are mad
Now you are seeing blue lights
Aliens and everything.
I heard the footsteps of the thief
Hurrying to make a jump
A flying exit
On the ground floor window
He took nothing important
Just made a total mess
And left a shoe on a pile of papers
He must have been a thief passionate of metaphors:
I stepped foot here in your privacy.

Years later, when my friend brought a pile of pancakes
I couldn't help it and I said in loud voice
Look: a tortoise
And I started laughing
I never chased to see things
Although I sometimes keep them silent
Or to laugh when I shouldn't laugh.
We discussed this over wine and laughter
Where does this laughter come from?
It's a way to break tension
You train everyday
So that when you really need it
You are prepared.
In times of drama, you give away the brightest laughter
Because this is what the incredible lightness of being is about.
When the man that called me mad left
I was laughing indeed like a madwoman
I almost said: I see a blue light.
Years after the thief passionate of symbols
Visited my house and my dreams
I realised I silently started becoming a thief myself
I enter people dreams
And steal away an unimportant thing
A little sparkle to put in a painting or a poem
Allowing them to go on waking up
In a new dream
And sneak away with a mad laughter
But not before
Blinding their dreams
With a blue light from a lighter
I always carry in my pocket.

THE PORTRAIT OF THE ARTIST AS A MONKEY HOPING TO GROW PEACOCK FEATHERS

You see those monkeys producing beautiful things
Let's let them suffer so they can produce some more
About loneliness
Destiny
And the meaning of life
Let's let them recreate
Life
Let's see those monkeys
Resembling peacocks
How they evolve to human
If they ever manage
To capture what life is about
Cause monkeys are the biggest losers or the biggest winners
They gamble everything
While sending love to the world from a tree.
They gamble everything
From true love to loneliness
Hoping that one day
Some true peacock feathers
Will grow in their tail.

They will leave the trail of their evolution
How sadness changed in tone and color
Marked on the coconut tree of life
Cause they believe life is about getting hit
By a coconut fallen from the tree of knowledge
And living to tell the story of this.
Don't laugh at monkeys
If you ever saw how hope looks on their face
The saddest thing
A monkey in love.

EVERYTHING COULD BE ILLUMINATED

Art is like a refugee camp
Where people withdraw when they become aware of the war they are part of
The private wars they were leading
Atrocious battle against oneself.
A refugee camp in which you arrive
And find out with surprise
You are not the only one.
Art is like a serene madhouse
In which the softer madmen go
The non aggressive ones
Those that would always turn with rage only against oneself.
You hear people singing
Birds singing
And wander if this is madness
Why is not everybody mad?
From time to time,
Nature produces unadapted individuals
That are meant to highlight that there is something wrong
With society nowadays
Or during those days

Or during the future days
Individuals that can see the bigger picture
As a landscape of time
That they see inside themselves.
If they are lucky enough they get inside a refugee camp
Or a serene madhouse
But most of them need to go on carrying that battle
On their own.

PASSION AND OTHER DEMONS

All artists want to get inside your soul
To move something there
A stone
Or a disguise.
The truth lies in a song
Sung in a language you do not understand
In an art you do not master
In the future you cannot grasp
In the past that today became a blurry memory
The warmth in your chest starts getting detached
The lie is for mortals
To feed passions with
But there is another warmth
It's universal.
If you ever visited the atelier of an old painter
You should know this
Because he says he does not do this
For the past
Or for the future
He says present tense does not matter
It's something else
A heart you cannot open every day
But it's the only one that matters

The universal heart.
You do not access it every day
It's something trembling
The core of humanity
Behind truth and lie
I see it with my eyes closed only
It could be somewhere lost in Arcadia
Last century Arcadia
Or next century Arcadia
Or Arcadia now
If you can grasp that
My dear.
Or in one of my photo collages in which I smile
I could be satisfied only in my imagination
Satisfied of grasping something universal
Like the meaning of a song
Sung in a language I do not understand.
The true light you can see only with your eyes closed
At night
The rest is just human lie.

THE TOWER

I have been building a tower
I started in a dream
With two stripes only
Pink and cerulean blue
And I went on building it
Like a sleepwalker, without knowing what I was doing
I built a tower out of air and transparencies
Trying to read the future on the other side of a sheet of paper you hold against the sun
A tower out of butterfly wings
Gold dust and longing.
I worked restlessly to built it
Touching the air with a brush I held in my heart shaped hands.
I had to be careful not to start flying
while building my tower
At the times when I still did not know what I was doing.
And when I knew
I had to be careful not to build it in the underground
Because one day I knew the gifts I was granted at birth need to be paid with loneliness
No matter how sad this may sound.
A sharp mind is a double sided knife

Cutting my own skin in search for purity
And the arches I use to conquer the world
Come back and hit my heart
Just like I would do with a butterfly I pin for my collection
Cause I had many hearts
And one of them was brave
And deserved a tower.
I built a tower for one mind only
In which to stand tall
And still
And travel the world with my eyes closed.
Only when the longing will stop, I will find peace
In the wings of a seagull I see at sunset from the last window of my tower
Peace is when you know that what is outside the tower is inside the tower as well
But still separated by some transparent walls made of butterfly wings.
Last night I finished my tower
I painted the last window in silence
A glass window that had the transparency of silence
Like when you look at the sea from behind a thick window and you don't hear anything.
I chose my palette carefully for the last window of my tower
Because I don't know what color
anger is
Since I never used it before
But eventually it has appeared on my palette
My tower has all the colors now
And it stands still, tall and transparent.
I painted the window and I closed it
And I started running on stairs

Slamming doors behind me.
I reached the top floor
I had gold dust on my shoulder
I will never know if I broke my own butterfly wings to build this
Or if this the only way to build beauty: out of sadness
Because at the top floor good and bad do not exist
I look outside, maybe I see peace in the wings of a seagull
And I breath silently.
If you will ever want to reach me, it's a very long way towards me now.

HEAD IN THE CLOUDS

I tried to do a self portrait
For the ten thousandth time
Capturing my essence is the hardest thing.
I did it in pencil on a white canvas
I said it's time to start over new.
But I could not keep an eye on myself
As I was watching the skies
Birds and clouds
I could be that as well.
I took a picture of the skies
Thinking about the difference between
One bird over clouds
And more birds over clouds.
This could be me split between birds and clouds
So I blended everything together
Like they used to blend everything together
In pots, in ancient times
A ritual of rebirth
The new woman
The essential woman.
I turned to digital art instead
To blend it together
And I shared it on facebook

Because I like sharing things.
I want to be immortal
My head in the clouds forever
A pot in the skies just like in ancient times
But I could be immortal if only time stops
Or if I manage to catch my essence in a self portrait
If I manage to count the numerous birds
From my head into clouds.
These birds were getting on my nerves
So I deleted my self portrait with fury
My left eye is distracted
And that is not even my nose
And this is not even my life
I have birds in my head
My head is in the clouds
Instead of being here, right here, right now.
I want to be immortal
But my self portrait in pencil does not exist anymore
And the birds I saw in the skies are long gone
So all I have left is a photograph
Damn digital art
This is the only way you can be immortal
In a photograph
The only way to stop time.
I have being dreaming uplately
Every night
About writing a line in a poem
And when I wake up it is gone
Maybe my essence is there
Hiding from me
No skies, no birds
Just unknown poetry.
I will keep looking for immortality

As long as I live
Watching life flowing in pictures of the skies
With one bird close to my eyebrow
And the others descending
To the land of dreams.

FLY AWAY MY BIRDS

I open the window and I say
Fly away my birds, fly away my poems
You are to prove a mathematical theory
That the sum of the vices
The sum of the feelings
The sum of loneliness
Is always constant.
And a loneliness is never equal to another loneliness.
Fly away my birds
Cause this is not your cage
There are 1001 eyes waiting to see
1001 shadows
In the sea of deaf ears
Sing to the outside world
Like all the mermaids
Sing in deep ocean
Cause what's outside is inside
It doesn't matter which way you set fire.
Fly away my birds
This time I am not flying with you
I will follow you in my dreams
Wearing my favorite shadow costume.
I will wait here in the kitchen

Sunk between knifes and brushes
Invoking the god of structure
To come back
Put structure to my thoughts
Bring me back to my golden cage
Although I now know
The brightest cage I carry inside.
I will wait here in the kitchen
Flying between knifes and brushes
Hoping for my hunger to stop
While deep frying in oil color
A bird of paradise.

UNDERSTANDING

A BIRD NAMED HOPE

If you would like to know what hope is
I would tell you this:
Hope is a bird.
Everybody carries a bird
And if you look attentively you sometimes see it
In people's eyes
You see it trembling and stretching.
With eyes wide open
We release a feather
Light as gold and heavy like a burden.
With arms stretched to the sky
As if flying was the most natural gesture
For bird carriers.
With eyes wide open and arms stretched to the sky
I raise a question
Light as gold and heavy as a feather:
Do you carry that bird
Or the bird carries you?
Will you cling to it or will you release it?
Will you fall
Or only then, when you let it go
A bird named hope will teach you how to fly.

IF ONE DAY, A MAN LOOKING LIKE JESUS*

If one day, a man looking like Jesus
Will just appear in your kitchen
With blue eyes and a thick beard
Or just a man that can see through your shyness
Or through your most outrageous acts
You know you will abandon yourself
You will kiss his forehead
And tremble a bit when his hands will first look for you.
You will abandon yourself
To your own lust
You will close your eyes and say
Look Jesus, I will teach you about faith
And eyes closed, you will give him all the love that others did not want
Cause my religion is passion
And my expectations are sky high
I have been waiting for you to save me
Since the first day I saw you
My grandma took me to meet you
In a countryside church
I remember your long hair and your thick beard
And your heavenly voice
In that little countryside church

Where you were performing an immemorial ritual
Just like the ritual we are performing now
Cause with my eyes closed, I remembered I know how to dance
The same dance our parents did
We are all looking for balance
And I was looking for you all these years
Cause look Jesus, you are immemorial
My animus
And now that I met you
Since you just appeared here in my kitchen
I should tell you there is no need to save me
Just kiss me
Cause I know that by the time I wake up, you will be gone.
And I will be gone also
Cause life is a journey
On the outside roads and on my inner paths
We travel by air, we navigate on rivers, we jump on night trains
We get stuck in train stations
And eventually we let go
All the pains heal
Even those electric ones that hindered us from walking
That kept us together until I abandoned myself.
We walk through time
In our hearts and on the outside
One cannot stop this flow
There is nothing that keeps me here anymore
Life will bring me other and other Jesuses
Cause my religion is passion
An insatiable faith.

In this poem I condensed most of the psychological knowledge that I have. It should not be taken literally. It refers to the so called 'animus' figure that Jung talks about in his psychology. It is a male image hidden in the soul of women, which should be integrated in the conscious personality in order to avoid its projections on persons we meet. The reference to Jesus is a personal touch because I believe people who are capable of much love end up becoming spiritual at some point in their lives.

FANTASY SUPPORTS FANTASY

I tried to imagine how the connections between people look like
Because I am sure we are all connected somehow
I saw a rope, a hook and some silk threads
And I saw Santa Claus
Swinging in my bathroom
Supported by another Santa Claus
Fantasy supports fantasy.
If there is a rope connecting two people
Attached to their wrists or to their necks
As long as they pull in the same direction
The rope is called comfort
And the rope meets its purpose
Because both Santa Clauses and two horses pulling the same carriage have a purpose.
When they start pulling in opposite directions
To avoid getting theirs wrists bruised
One needs something strong to cut off the rope
Such as some irons scissors or will
And the half rope you end up with, you can start calling it hope.
There are some connection stronger then the rope
The iron hook connection

What pirates with former bruised wrists used to wear
To replace their hands.
When people cling to each other
With all their being: flesh and blood and hook shaped hands
Cutting the connection is very painful
Invoking all the ghost pains that pirates feel in their missing hands.
One might think the pirates connections are the hardest to break
But then you have the silk threads.
Imagine a silk scarf,
Light, colorful
With many knots on it
A scarf that cannot keep you warm
That cannot meet a purpose of comfort
But silk threads are the strongest
They do no burn, they do not break
There is a worm producing beauty
Just give him a helpful pirate hand
Adding some knots to its slippery surface
Trying to push the chord
To see how much can beauty withstand.
But the most durable connection between beings
Is in my bathroom
Santa Claus sitting on a swing
Legs balancing over the void
And another Santa Claus supporting him
Fantasy supports fantasy
With a helpful pirate hand holding the silk ropes
Making the world
Swing back and forth
Cause that is the key for balance: to keep moving.

COLORS

THE COLOR OF YOUR BEING

Imagine your body doubled by something else
That has the consistency of fog
Imagine your hands transparent
So you can see that fog we all carry inside
For me it is pale blue
Or sometimes lila.
Imagine a cry and its color
And remember a cry means both a tear and a yell,
Imagine the color of silence
And the effect on the fog we all carry inside
You never know where it went
If silence installed in your chest
Or in your heel
If it can be healed or not.
Imagine a storm inside fog
And how it changes the color of your being
Remember that not all people see the colors in the same way
It is a matter of sensibility
Indeed.
And a storm inside pale blue,
That is the color of the fog I carry inside
Which I could see if my hands were transparent,

Could move away some currents
Which for me are deep blue.
I believe I was born in deep blue
I carry a stone which I don't know whom it belongs to.
Imagine that all the people that you met in your life
Left a hole in your being,
That has the consistency of fog,
And that other people came
To cover those holes
To unify the color of your being
To make it shiny a bit
Like sun falling over fog
And then they made new wounds.
Imagine that people do not die of old age
But because they have too many holes in their foggy being,
That lila
Or pale blue
Lost shininess.
And imagine me
Rising a stone.
Imagine the storm inside fog that goes with it
And remember I never liked faint colors
I always looked for purity
And deep meaning
The true color of my being
May be different
I was born in deep blue.

ONE LITTLE MAN ESCAPED MY RIGHT HAND

My emotions do not circulate well inside my body
I spotted seven little men going up and down
One of them put a chair behind my eyes
And just sits there, observing the horizon
He says he is in charge, but sometimes he falls asleep
The others keep making noise
I told them to behave, I threatened them with yoga
I said
This is the upwards direction, from my core to the head and outside
And this is the downwards direction,
we check what that little man on his chair says and we react accordingly
We all go down to the core now and everything is fine.
But no,
Sometimes they go outside my ears and scare old ladies on the streets
They go to my mouth
And to my hands
And keep doing things not all of us agree.
One day, one little man went to my right hand
He said he has something to deliver and went outside

He never came back
And we did a little council today to agree upon sending a little man to look for him
But we never agree on anything
Anyway.

COLORFUL RAIN

This is precisely how I feel today
Colors dripping from my soul
Blinded by the white
Unadapted to cold
And to many other things.
I feel like a feelings hunter,
A bit guilty,
Hiding away treasures
Cause I hid many things in this painting.
I brought unintentional colored rain to the world
And this is even stranger
Cause this is precisely how I feel today
I have been hunting my feelings
At least to know what to kill
Before they start haunting me.
And I ended up with colorful rain
Staining the world
Now try to catch colorful rain and try to kill it.

COLOR ORACLE

I have been riding on an emotional roller coaster up lately
I want to get off
And I know a staircase from roller coasters to earth
It's called sincerity
Accepting the part of the truth I refused to think of
I should say it again
In capital letters
Write it in red paint over my hands on a canvas
No one is responsible for your happiness
And ultimately no one is responsible for your misery
For your roller coaster rides.
But what is a magician supposed to do
When past and future get condensed on my canvas
I use a color oracle
To guess what life is about
My hands everyday stained with different colors
I guess my moods
And the ones of others
I am an over sensitive magician
Cause I know things
How can a magician explain all these
I just know
Without the color oracle.

I do all this
So that you know that I know.
When one bathes in the deepest waters
Or goes flying in the skies
You and I dissolve
It becomes us.
Us all.
And go ahead
Call me mad
But I have proofs
All the canvases I stained
Before staining my hands with sincerity
But it is not staining
It's called the art of divination in us all.
I am an over sensitive magician
That sometimes gets tired
Cause even magicians sometimes need to take a rest
Or should I say magicians are especially those
That need to go on holiday
From themselves.
I should write that in red paint
On my hands:
No one is responsible for your
happiness.
And get off the emotional roller coaster
Cause magicians are those that get often lost
In present tense
They mix persons
They say you
When they mean I
And go on guessing
In that color oracle.
I wrote the story of my life

In red paint
On a canvas depicting my hands
Or your hands
Or whoever I was guessing about
In my color oracle.
And now that I wrote it
I should look for that staircase
Named sincerity
And go outside and live it.
The end.

FORGIVE

BREAK THE WEAKNESS CHAIN WITH BEAUTY

I remember
It was a rainy spring day
And I skipped school to go meet him.
My favourite month is May in Bucharest
It smells like flowers everywhere.
It was raining and my umbrella was broken
Looking like a dead bat wing.
He was an art school student and tried to teach me about joy
He introduced me to his professor:
She is an artist.
But I was only an artist of criticism back then
Specialised in bitterness and cryptic poems.
I remember him feeding the cats
from the fourth floor window,
His legs balancing over the void,
Me horrified and him laughing.
I remember carrying water in my shoes all day
And his hands recalling a forgotten rhythm on my ribs
Trying again to teach to me about joy.
But I had a golden cage inside my chest
And I still have it

Although now I think I might actually have
More golden cages inside myself.
I remember a picture taken on a street in Bucharest in May
A picture smelling like flowers
Possibility of joy and refusals
Cause after we sat on a couch in the middle of the street
Me, his friends and him,
Me looking almost transparent
Like a ghost incapable of absorbing joy,
Cause after we sat on a couch in the middle of the street
For a picture destined to smell like flowers
Some of us looking bright
And some looking transparent,
I ruined everything.
I started feeding the void, instead of feeding cats
From the fourth floor window.
He never spoke to me again
But I once met him by chance
He said he recognised my voice and my laughter
Crystal clear
I tried to grab his hand
Check if you recall that rhythm on my ribs now
Check which golden cage is smelling like flowers.
But memory is a transparent thing
And I never had the chance to apologise
For feeding the void, instead of feeding cats
From the fourth floor window.
Everything we live goes into compartments
Separated by thick or thin walls
Sometimes transparent,
But today I burst into tears
Thinking about Frieda Khalo's

watermelon
About how I ended up teaching joy myself
Cause back then I was just an artist of criticism.
I think one of the transparent walls broke
Cause I heard glass breaking
Crystal clear.
And I feel wind blowing between the compartments
A spring wind
Smelling like flowers
Reminding me that this is the rhythm of life
And I can fully recall it now.
This painting is about a weakness chain
And I did it after I saw a theatre play about madmen
Thinking that this is why they chose to be actors
So they could be madmen on stage
For two hours.
This could be the weakness chain
About people hurting others
And so on
Ad infinitum
But now I know something new
That the difference between an artist and a madman is strength
The strength to be who you are
In front of others
But especially in front of yourself
The strength to break the walls
Between the golden cages you carry inside
And let go
Flying to the world
A poem of apology,
Break the weakness chain with beauty.

LOVE AND LAVA

The lines on the inside of my hands do not match
Although they should
Just like for many years
The inside did not match the outside
I kept hiding
Behind my fingers
I was afraid of who was standing behind
But I remember in that afternoon
I was trembling
And it was not because of the cold
There was an earthquake happening inside
And just like during all the earthquakes
The grounds rearranged
And lava started coming out
Everything shaking and burning
And now I sit here looking at my hands
Releasing passion to the world
Cause love and lava are close to madness and obsession
And if one day I will be close to saying
I was turning mad and you just turned your back
I will remember that I sit here
Releasing passion to the world
Because I experienced warmth

And I stand on different grounds now
Because during an earthquake
That you might have mistaken for cold
They rearranged.
I am not scared of who was hiding behind my hands
Anymore
Although sometimes the intensity of this passion is frightening
I will follow the shock waves engraved on my palms.

SOLACE

STAY TRUE TO YOURSELF

Stay true to yourself
Just like you are
Moody, volatile, exaggerated
Cause one day you will collect the flowers grown from the seeds you planted.
Stay true to yourself
And do not bend down
In front of transitory winds
You are wind yourself
And fire and heat
And water and depth
You are your land
The ground of your own emotions.
Let go in front of them
And you will find that wind slowly
Becoming a normal breath inside your body.
Stay true to yourself
Even if you are both fact and fiction
You plant imaginary seeds
But you can grow real flowers.
Think about love as a balance
The love to the world that you give
And the need to feel loved

The need for heat and depth grounding your body to the wind
That is the life that you are breathing.
Stay true to yourself
And one day you will find yourself climbing stairs
With the most elastic style of walking
You did not think you are capable of.
You might be even climbing stars
in a sunny day that comes after all
the lunatic visions.
You are both sun and moon
And this is what staying true to yourself is about.

LET'S MEET ON THE BACK OF THE MONSTER

Let's meet on the back of the monster
As if meeting on the bridge between fact and fiction
Let's meet and imagine the best strategy
To tame that monster
Because I've heard that ages ago
There were people
Who managed to tame wolves and lions.
Let's meet on the back of the old monster
That every generation tried to tame
And let us be the first who manage
To breed dogs, cats and some other creatures
I still do not know how to call.

THE DAY I REMEMBERED I AM FREE TO FEEL WHATEVER I LIKE

If one day you discover joy
Hidden in tubes and splashes of color
Don't try to become the master of joy.
Learning the technique of joy
Is like putting structure into your emotions
Like drawing lines between this and that
Between how it is and how it should be
When emotions are supposed to mingle.
When you choose a color
You're not hiding the opposite
They live peacefully together.
I don't want to be the master of joy anymore
I just want to feel it
In peace with myself and the rainbow of emotions.
This is not a poem
Although it has these strange breaks at the end of the row
And this is not a painting
It's just joy splashed on canvas
The day I remembered I am free to feel whatever I like.

THE DELICATE MECHANISM

There is something happening with me up lately
I don't know if to call it madness of purity of emotion
I thought it's because of the puppies I am taking care of
Or because I set my painting free once again.
I listened to my heart ticking,
A delicate mechanism,
I thought about blue entering and red leaving
Like in those anatomical diagrams
And then I rushed outside to see the sunset
A magnificent sunset
For two days in a row.
I thought about the heart,
This delicate mechanism,
As long as it is ticking
It cannot be broken.
I put some blue and red on a canvas
And then I looked at my heart
Colored like the sunset.
I saw some wings covering a puppy
Protecting a delicate mechanism
I looked at my heart ticking on a canvas
Flying over sunset
And I started laughing out loud

You, mad girl
You fell in love again
With life.

YIN AND YANG

I was sitting in my room thinking about yin and yang
This circle, half black, half white with small circles inside
of the opposite strength or weakness
Because inside of strength you have weakness
And inside of weakness you have strength
Chaos as weakness and order as strength
And you can rotate it clockwise or counter-clockwise
Slowly or faster.
Just like when I went outside on a sunny day and I squeezed my eyes
Unadapted to light anymore
And I realised I have been living like an owl for months now
But in the dark I see so well, my eyes getting bigger and more
conscious of that little spot of white
Sparkling
A solitary star sparkling while the skyline is slowly rotating
Clockwise or counter-clockwise.
Or just like when I got upset that no one reads my poetry
Pages and pages of useless records of that slowly rotating motion

But then on the white side I realised that at least I wrote something not to be read
This is the strong half of the circle with a dark spot of vanity inside.
And when I say poetry, I mean these texts with strange breaks at the end of the row
And their only purpose is to mark the rhythm of that slow rotation from
black to white
Because nothing happened, I just had the time to study that yin and yang circle
From the top and from the bottom
From a time wise perspective.
One evening, I was on the white side of the circle
Either on the half or only on the spot
I couldn't tell because this wheel of fortune keeps spinning
Uncontrollable
But still observable.
My big owl eyes got distracted by something on national geographic wild
And I started getting excited again
Like I could get only in a botanical garden resembling a jungle
Or inside a museum.
I got excited because of a little horse
Not a pony, just a horse in miniature
That remains in adult age at the size of a big dog
A little horse that was strangely enough black and white
And I could feed him carrots and stories
And walk around together by foot or by bus
Or even by plane
Saying:

This is me and this is my horse.
Allowing my inner voice to speak loudly
Cause this what I learnt while studying the black and white circle
My inner voice should speak even if this means releasing a torrent.
I remember I was once in a museum in Den Haag
And they were saying they had this commission with an artist to give them every print of the artwork he produces
When he reached 3000 they had to stop
I won't tell you the name of that artist cause you might suspect me of vanity
When I have just a rich inner voice with a dark spot on it.
And I remember also reading a text of Julio Cortazar
About excitement
Going to the theatre and getting over emotional and marvelling at
everything
And feeling like an idiot when he was told it was, well, not that special
He agreed with them
But only until the next time he got excited.
Because the wheel keeps turning
And it's even better if it rotates with a black and white horse on top of it.

THIS IS MY PERSONAL WARMTH

In poetry and in painting
Just like in your dreams
You can do whatever you please
You can write inside a landscape
With golden shadows at sunset over a forest:
This is my personal warmth
I tried to hide it for many years.
You can write over the fur of a dog
Inside a forest at sunset
I have the heart of a dog
And I liked felines all my life.
You can write out of the blue
On a sky you must have dreamt of
I appreciate kindness
Because I believe that is greatest virtue
And it took me many years of flying around
Suspended inside my protective cover
To understand
The redundancy of that sign saying leave the dog alone.
I find my warmth intact
And those who are familiar with
Poetry, painting and flying
Will understand this.

ABOUT THE AUTHOR

Laura Livia Grigore is a poet, painter and psychology enthusiast, with a background in space engineering. She likes to experiment with various mediums and types of writing. Her artwork is orientated on emotions, reflecting her opinion that most of the answers we need can be found inside ourselves, although the hardest thing to do is to be sincere with oneself. She is constantly looking for purity and the meaning of everything we live. Her search for freedom is reflected in the desire to experiment in her artwork. She believes that every person can find peace and satisfaction by practising an art, whether painting, writing, dancing, acting or anything else, and one can always find the time for this, despite the tiring and repetitive 9 to 5 life. She also considers that as technology advances, the creativity of people will increase, if they are wise enough to unleash the tremendous healing power of art and listen to their true inner voice.

Visit Laura on Facebook and on her website:

https://www.facebook.com/paintingsandadventures

www.paintingsandadventures.wordpress.com

Printed in Great Britain
by Amazon